SUBMARINE WARFARE

• AN ILLUSTRATED HISTORY •

ANTONY PRESTON

Thunder Bay
P·R·E·S·S

This edition published in 1999 by
Thunder Bay Press
5880 Oberlin Drive, Suite 400
San Diego, CA 92121-4794
1-800-2846-3580
http://www.advmkt.com

Library of Congress Cataloging-in-Publication Data

Preston, Antony, 1938-
Submarine warfare / Antony Preston.
p.   cm.
Includes index.
ISBN 1-57145-172-2
1. Submarine warfare.   2. Submarines (Ships)--History.   I. Title.
V210.P67   1998
359.9'3--dc21   99-11910
CIP

Editor: *Anne Cree*
Design: *Wilson Design Associates*
Picture Research: *Antony Preston and Ken Botham*

Printed in The Czech Republic

Picture credits:
via Antony Preston: 6, 10, 11, 12, 15, 16, 19, 26,
40-41, 46, 47, 49, 55, 60, 61, 72, 73, 87, 90, 95, 96,
97, 101, 102, 103, 108-109, 121, 131, 132, 133,
139, 140, 141, 142
TRH Pictures: 2-3, 9 (both), 13, 20, 23, 24, 27, 28,
29, 32, 33, 35, 38-39, 42, 45, 48, 50 (both), 51, 53,
54, 58, 62, 64, 66 (both), 67, 69, 70, 71, 76-77, 78,
84, 86, 88, 91, 92-93, 94, 104, 106, 109, 111, 112,
113, 114, 115, 116, 117, 118-119, 120, 122,
124, 125, 126-127, 128, 130, 135, 137, 138-139,
back cover
Artwork credits:
Aerospace Publishing: 18, 25, 31, 36, 37, 41, 44, 56,
65 (both), 71, 74, 75, 82, 83, 92, 110, 123
Istituto Geografico De Agostini S.p.A.: 12, 14-15,
17, 22-23, 24-25, 26, 28, 30, 46-47, 51, 52 (both),
68-69, 98-99, 112-113

Contents

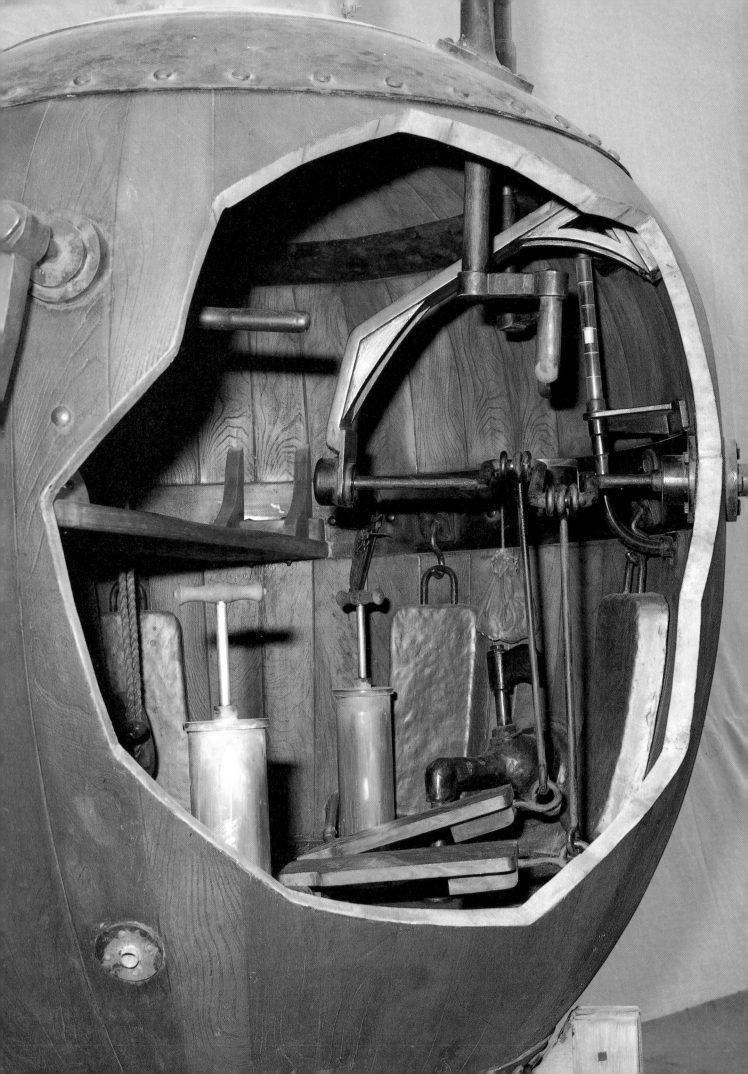

CHAPTER ONE

Early Submarines

The submarine had been a dream of inventors for centuries, but only became a practical possibility in the last century. Even in the last years of the nineteenth century it was still little more than an expensive toy, more dangerous to its operators than its enemies. That said, navies were quick to appreciate the submarine's potential.

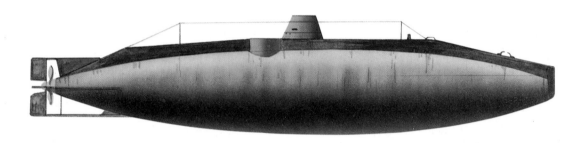

The lure of underwater travel seems to have obsessed inventors almost as much as the wish to fly, but the first attempt to address practical problems did not come until the sixteenth century. In 1578 an Englishman called William Bourne wrote of a submersible boat in his book *Inventions and Devices*. Although there is no evidence that Bourne built such a boat, he clearly grasped the essentials: a watertight hull, ballast tanks and a means of expelling the seawater from those tanks to return to the surface. He described a wooden hull, with leather bags in the bilges which would be filled with seawater through holes in the side of the boat, destroying its positive buoyancy. To return to the surface two screw presses would squeeze the

Left: A reconstruction of David Bushnell's *Turtle*, using the designer's description as a basis, showed it to be well engineered and practical, though very tiring to operate.

water out again, restoring buoyancy. He also proposed a hollow mast to refresh the air supply.

There were, however, drawbacks to this idea. Bourne is silent on the subject of propulsion, but it can be assumed that he intended his submersible to be propelled by oars. As later inventors were to discover, even an air mast could not provide sufficient oxygen for the exhausted rower. Nor is there any mention of a purpose, warlike or peaceful, for the invention. If warlike, there was no means of attacking a hostile ship.

In 1624 a Dutch physician, Cornelius van Drebbel, went to England to demonstrate two examples of his design. Unlike Bourne, he relied only on oars to force his boat to dive, an even more exhausting procedure. He is reputed to have persuaded King James I to embark on an underwater trip, but claims of a trip lasting several hours can be dismissed as wild exaggeration. During the next century submarine

Above: Robert Fulton's *Nautilus* under sail on the surface (top) and running submerged (below). Unlike the *Turtle*, the *Nautilus* saw no action.

inventors proliferated. Some were clearly charlatans, but others were obsessed – often to a suicidal degree. In 1773 a ship's carpenter called Day achieved a successful dive in Plymouth Sound, using a novel system of detachable ballast in the form of boulders hung externally. Sadly, his second dive in June 1774 ended in disaster when the hull collapsed at a depth of 40.3m (132.2ft). Lord Sandwich, the First Lord of the Admiralty, was visiting Plymouth at the time and ordered the Royal Navy to attempt a salvage operation, the first ever.

A CRUDE TOY

The War of Independence in America inspired a young Yale graduate, David Bushnell, to build a 'sub-marine vessel' to break the Royal Navy blockade of the rebel colonies' harbours. His *Turtle* was an egg-shaped wooden hull with room for one operator, who worked a rudder and a screw propeller. Two pumps allowed water ballast to be expelled, and the operator was also able to manoeuvre a vertical screw to attach a gunpowder charge to the keel of an enemy ship. Although the tiny submersible did not survive the war, Bushnell wrote a detailed explanation for Thomas Jefferson in 1787, which was sufficient for the Smithsonian Institution to make an accurate model 200 years later.

The *Turtle* made history by carrying out the first underwater war mission, when in September 1776 an army sergeant named Ezra Lee paddled down the Hudson River to attack Lord Howe's flagship, the 64-gun HMS *Eagle*. Lee located his target and struggled valiantly to attach the explosive charge to her keel, but the screw broke, and Lee was forced to work his way back upriver. It was assumed at the time that the coppering on the keel of the *Eagle* prevented the screw from penetrating, and for 200 years this theory went unchallenged. Modern research into Admiralty records shows, however, that HMS *Eagle* had no coppering applied to her underwater hull until a considerable time later. This leaves only two explanations: the first is that Ezra Lee encountered iron fastenings, perhaps near the rudder; the second is that he was suffering from the narcotic effects of breathing his own air for too long. The lethargy, combined with physical exhaustion, would, in the opinion of modern divers, have been sufficient to discourage the gallant sergeant.

Two further attacks by the *Turtle* were made later, but with no success, and the tiny craft was finally lost while being transported in a frigate which ran aground. Another American, Robert Fulton, took the submarine story further. Unlike Bushnell, he was an ardent pacifist who wanted to destroy warships and so rid the world of expensive and repressive armaments. Like many idealists he looked to the French Revolution to provide a new world order, but the near-bankrupt Directory could not afford the price of Fulton's scheme to annihilate the Royal Navy. The disgusted inventor took his idea to Holland, but the thrifty burghers were not happy to pay the high price asked. Two years later he returned to France, and compromised with his principles to the extent of selling his design to Napoleon, the man who used French military might to subjugate Europe. With financial backing from the First Consul work could start, and in the spring of 1800 Fulton's boat was launched as the *Nautilus*.

The new submersible was much bigger than the *Turtle*, a cylindrical copper hull on iron framing. The crew of three would still have to row the *Nautilus*, but she was given a small sail to reduce the strain during surface running. After several dives in the Seine the *Nautilus* was sent to Brest, where the Maritime Prefect found the prospect of submarine warfare too inhumane. Faced with Fulton's exorbitant demands and unsubstantiated claims of attacks on British ships, the French began to suspect that they were dealing with a fraudster. Their suspicions seem justified because in 1804

Above: Wilhelm Bauer's *Brandtaucher* helped to break a Danish blockade in 1850, but sank a month later. He went on to design a British submarine to fight in the Crimean War.

Right: The Confederate CSS *Hunley* sinking the frigate USS *Housatonic* with a spar torpedo, February 1864. Years later the *Hunley* was discovered near the wreck of her victim.

Fulton went to London to try to sell his secret to the British Prime Minister, William Pitt. Although he blew up a brig convincingly the Admiralty set its face against any dealings with the American inventor. Lord St Vincent denounced Pitt as 'the greatest fool that ever existed to encourage a mode of warfare which those who commanded the sea did not want, and which, if successful, would deprive them of it'.

Although the old seadog's opinion has been widely seen as reactionary and stupid, he turned out to be right. The submarine was still too crude to influence naval warfare. Until some form of safe mechanical propulsion – and something more effective than a keg of gunpowder with a clockwork fuse – were available, the submarine was doomed to remain a toy, more lethal to its operator than the enemy.

Submarine inventors appear to have gone very quiet during the long peace after the Napoleonic Wars, but in 1850, when war broke out between Denmark and Prussia, a Bavarian artillery sergeant called Wilhelm Bauer came up with an idea to break the Danish blockade of Kiel. His submarine, named *Brandtaucher*

('Fire Diver'), was a rectangular sheet metal tank propelled by a handwheel. Water ballast was taken in to dive, but underwater manoeuvring was done by moving a heavy weight forwards and backwards.

The *Brandtaucher*'s first dive at the end of 1850 was successful, causing the Danish blockade to be lifted, but little more than a month later disaster struck. While diving in Kiel harbour at a depth of 60m (196.8ft) the plating at the stern collapsed, taking the little submarine to the bottom. Bauer had a cool head, however, and told the two sailors to allow the boat to flood, raising the air pressure sufficiently to

Above: Simon Lake's *Argonaut* was a wooden-hulled prototype built at his own expense to demonstrate the idea of running on the seabed; the US Navy was not impressed.

blow the hatches open. He calmed their panic, and five hours later all three floated to the surface, the first submariners ever to escape from a sunken submarine.

Like all good inventors Bauer was not deterred by the setback, and during the Crimean War went to England to sell his ideas to the Royal Navy. The new Prime Minister, Lord Palmerston, sanctioned the expenditure of £7000 to build a prototype. But there the trail grows cold, for although Admiral Sir Astley Cooper-Key recalled seeing it, and a contract was apparently placed with a Liverpool shipyard, no technical details have survived. Cooper-Key described it as a large diving bell which could be walked along the seabed by its operators – hardly a submarine and having nothing in common with Bauer's earlier ideas.

The likeliest explanation is that the prototype existed, but the British Government exaggerated its capabilities to frighten the Russians. This infers that 'Lord Palmerston's Submarine' never got beyond the drawing board, or was never completed, possibly because of technical or contractual problems. Bauer offered the Russians a design called the *Seeteufel* ('Sea Devil') in 1855, and in 1856 she is reported to have embarked several musicians at Kronstadt to play the National Anthem during Tsar Alexander II's coronation. In a 17.8m (58.4ft) hull the noise must have been deafening – and likely to use up oxygen even faster than usual.

After the brief Anglo-French alliance against Russia the peace saw a return to normality, with the French trying to overcome British naval supremacy. This time the inventor was a Captain Bourgois, who submitted proposals for a submersible. Five years later his *Plongeur* was launched at Rochefort, a comparatively large 44.5m (145.9ft) boat driven by a steam engine to provide compressed air for expelling water ballast, as well as propulsion. The weapon was a spar torpedo – a canister of gunpowder on a long wooden pole, intended to be driven against an enemy ship's side before being detonated.

THE AMERICAN CIVIL WAR

Although the *Plongeur*'s design took submarine development forward, the 'enabling technologies' were not yet mature. The compressed air reservoirs could not hold sufficient pressure, and the spar torpedo, if successful, was virtually guaranteed to sink the attacker as well. This kamikaze weapon was the fatal flaw in the primitive submarines developed by the Confederacy in the American Civil War. The first *David* (so named because it was seen as a giant-killer), was more of a semi-submersible torpedo boat than a true submarine, a steam-propelled vessel capable of being trimmed down to reduce the risk of being spotted at night. This was essential because the target ship could all too easily prevent the *David* from getting close enough to use the spar torpedo, either by evasive action or by gunfire.

The prototype *David* was swamped by the wash of a passing steamer, but was raised and manned by a new volunteer crew. In October 1863, off Charleston, she damaged the Union ironclad *New Ironsides* but took virtually all her crew down with her. A more advanced design was produced by Horace L Hunley four months later, and built at Mobile, Alabama. Despite reverting to a hand crank for propulsion, *Hunley*'s 19m (62.3ft) craft was closer to a true submersible, although it is unlikely that she could do more than dip beneath the surface for short periods. She was, however, very dangerous, and sank three times, killing 23 men including her inventor. Raised for the fourth time, she was named CSS *Hunley* in honour of her designer and put under the command of Lt George Dixon of the Alabama Light Infantry, with a crew of eight volunteers.

On the night of 17 February 1864 the little submersible headed towards the new Union frigate USS *Housatonic*. Although sighted by the frigate's lookouts the *Hunley* had come too close, and from the forward hatch Dixon pulled the lanyard to fire the charge of the spar torpedo. A huge explosion lifted the

Housatonic from the water and within minutes she sank by the stern, the first ship ever to be sunk by a submarine in combat. But mystery surrounded the fate of the *Hunley*, for it was believed that she had made her escape, but many years later the wreck of the tiny cigar-shaped submersible was discovered close to the *Housatonic*. She had been swamped by the wave created by the explosion, and eight skeletons were found, still seated along the crankshaft. Recently the wreck has been raised to study details of the design and to try to restore her as a museum exhibit.

The Union Navy had no need for submersibles because it controlled the coastal waters and the rivers of the Confederacy, but public alarm at the exploits of the *David*s and the *Hunley* forced the Federal Government to make some sort of riposte. A French design from Brutus de Villeroi was built and named *Alligator*, but she sank in tow off Cape Hatteras in 1863. The *Intelligent Whale*, built in 1864 to a design by Oliver Halstead, resembled the *Hunley* in being hand-cranked, but the whale shape of the hull was much more efficient. She was too late for the war but her hull is still preserved at Washington Navy Yard.

TORPEDOES

The patchy performance of submersibles in the Civil War did nothing to quench the designers' enthusiasm. In 1878 the Reverend George Garrett registered a patent for 'Improvements in and Appertaining to Submarine or Subaqueous Boats or Vessels for Removing, Destroying, Laying or Placing Torpedoes in Channels and other Situations and for other Purposes' and established the Garrett Submarine Navigation and Pneumataphore Company Limited in London.

The reference to torpedoes echoes the experiences of the Civil War, in which Confederate moored mines had scored some successes against Union warships. Clearly, the Whitehead 'automobile' torpedo was considered too expensive or not yet reliable. At this time the term 'torpedo', (which took its name from an electric ray which stuns its prey), applied to all underwater weapons whether moored, towed or self-propelled. Only later would the 'tin fish' and the mine become separate.

GARRETT'S *RESURGAM*

Garrett's 4.4m (14.4ft) *Resurgam* ('I shall rise') dived by the movement of a piston permitting seawater to enter the hull. Propulsion was still by a hand crank, but in spite of this limitation the boat proved sufficiently successful for a second prototype to be built in 1879. The 30.48 tonne (30-ton), 21.5m (70.5ft) *Resurgam II* adopted steam propulsion, using an engine based on the Lamm 'fireless' principle, used to power London Underground Railway locomotives among others. Steam was generated by a large coal-fired boiler on the surface and stored in a tank, to be released when the submarine dived. The steam was sufficient to drive the submarine for four hours at two to three knots. The boat

Below: The Revd George Garrett poses with his baby son on the conning tower of his second prototype, *Resurgam II*, at the Birkenhead shipyard of Charles Cochrane & Co.

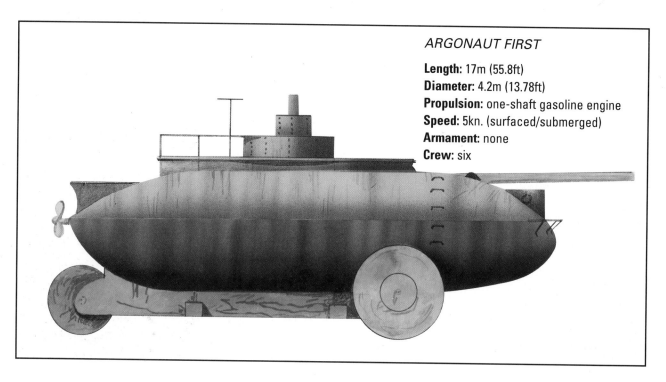

ARGONAUT FIRST

Length: 17m (55.8ft)
Diameter: 4.2m (13.78ft)
Propulsion: one-shaft gasoline engine
Speed: 5kn. (surfaced/submerged)
Armament: none
Crew: six

Above: Simon Lake's first full-scale submarine had no electric motor or batteries, but exhausted the lethal petrol fumes through a tall air-mast, a forerunner of the snorkel.

Below: Lake's *Argonaut First* at sea, probably in 1898, just after completion. Successful trials led to a number of export orders, but he had already lost the initiative to John Holland in the eyes of the US Navy.

started trials in December 1879, but was lost in tow on 26 February 1880 off the Welsh coast.

Garrett had already intended to demonstrate his submarine to the rich Swedish inventor Thorsten Nordenfelt, and the loss of *Resurgam II* proved no setback. Nordenfelt put up fresh capital to finance the construction of a much larger prototype, *Nordenfelt No.1* at Stockholm. The 30.2m (99ft) hull was capable of diving to just over 23m (75.4ft), using a steam engine similar to that in *Resurgam II*, and was armed with an external Whitehead torpedo-tube. Laid down in 1882, she ran trials at Landskrona three years later before being sold to Greece. Predictably, Turkey became alarmed and responded by ordering two more in 1886. These two, named *Abdul Mejid* and *Abdul Hamid*, were built at Chertsey on the River Thames and then shipped in sections to Constantinople for reassembly under Garrett's supervision. They were driven by Franq engines working on similar principles to the Lamm engine in *Resurgam II*, and in addition to a single torpedo-tube on the forward casing, had a Nordenfelt machine gun abaft the funnel.

Like most early submarines the Turkish models lacked longitudinal stability, and the Turkish Navy found difficulty in persuading anyone to volunteer to serve in them. Both were laid up ashore at the Golden Horn, and when a German technical mission inspected them in 1914 they were rusted beyond recognition.

The fourth Garrett-Nordenfelt design was much more ambitious: a 59m (193.5ft) boat displacing 249 tonnes

(245 tons) submerged. She was built as a speculative venture by the Barrow Shipbuilding Company (later Vickers) at Barrow-in-Furness and launched in 1887 in time to appear at Queen Victoria's Golden Jubilee Review at Spithead. The Tsar of Russia was duly impressed and ordered his ministers to buy the submarine. In November 1888 she left for Kronstadt escorted by the yacht *Lodestar*, but ran aground off the Jutland coast in Denmark. Although the hull was refloated the Russian government refused to accept her, and it was left to the insurers to reimburse the builders. Thereafter, Garrett and Nordenfelt parted company, the former to drift into obscurity and the latter to continue as a successful engineer, but not in the submarine field. Rumours of two more Nordenfelt boats built at Kiel and Danzig in 1891 are not supported by modern research.

A 'SALT WATER ENTERPRISE'

In parallel with Garrett's early efforts a group of Irish-Americans on the other side of the Atlantic were embarking on an enterprise which would ultimately make history. The Fenian United Brotherhood hatched secret plans for a 'Salt Water Enterprise', a submarine boat capable of striking what was hoped would be a mortal blow to British maritime power. The Brotherhood's 'Skirmishing Fund' first invested in a 6.8m (22.3ft) submersible designed by an unknown Irish-American inventor called John P. Holland. His prototype (designated by historians *Holland I*) was a modest success, although his far-

Above: Holland's sixth design was built as a private venture and accepted into service as the USS *Holland* (later designated SS-1) after successful sea trials.

sighted faith in the petrol-driven internal combustion engine proved premature, and the petrol engine was converted to steam. Heartened by this success the controllers of the 'Skirmishing Fund' provided $20,000 to build the so-called *Fenian Ram* (a name bestowed by the press, and chronologically known as *Holland II*). The boat was ordered in secret from the Delamater Ironworks in New York. After many squabbles work began in May 1879, but the 14.6m (48ft) boat was not launched until May 1881. It was driven by a Brayford two-cylinder double-acting petrol engine, a great improvement in power : weight ratio, and was armed with a pneumatic gun forward, firing at an upward angle.

The new submarine's existence was a poorly kept secret and many foreign visitors were shown around, although Holland refused to allow journalists to examine the interior. The *Fenian Ram* performed well, proving robust and reasonably safe. Unfortunately, internal dissent led some of the leading Fenians to seize the submarine to try to carry out a pre-emptive attack on the British, but they ran the little submarine ashore. She was salvaged but never went to sea again; in 1916 she was exhibited to raise funds for Irish independence and was later preserved as a memorial. Renovation has started recently.

John Holland's zeal for the Fenian cause waned after the failure of the midget Fenian Model of 1883 (*Holland III*), and henceforward he was to devote his energy to selling his designs. Brief but unhappy dealings with Captain Edward Zalinski resulted in a wooden-hulled boat armed with Zalinski's Dynamite Gun (*Holland IV*). Badly damaged at her launch in 1885, she soon passed into obscurity.

EUROPE – SEEDBED OF SUCCESS

We leave Holland for the moment, frustrated in his efforts to find a financial backer. It must have been galling to read of European and American rivals winning credit for what were, in his eyes, inferior designs. Everybody was trying to build a submarine, ranging from small *Turtle*-sized craft to 63.5m (208.3ft) monsters. Space does not permit a list of all the experiments, but one stands out. In 1886 a young Spanish naval officer, Isaac Peral, designed a submarine for the Spanish Navy, driven by two 30hp electric motors using current from a 420-cell accumulator battery. Although the boat was built, and named *Peral* in honour of her designer, the Spanish Navy was in no position to develop such advanced technology and early electricity generators and accumulator batteries were very heavy.

France was bound to be the seedbed of success; the Jeune Ecole theorists were looking for an 'equaliser' to get around the fact that the Royal Navy was much more powerful than its French rival. French engineers had made significant progress in the design of electric motors, and were able to improve on the ideas of Isaac Peral and solve some of the major technical problems. The famous naval architect, Dupuy de Lôme, lent his prestige to a design from Gustave Zédé, the 17.8m (58.4ft) *Gymnote* (Eel). Although small, the *Gymnote*'s 55hp electric motor could drive her at 6 knots, using current from 564 lead-acid accumulator batteries.

The little submarine created a sensation when she appeared in 1888, and despite her numerous shortcomings she pointed the way ahead. The Minister of Marine ordered Zédé's successor at Toulon Dockyard, Gaston Romazotti, to design a larger submarine to incorporate the lessons. Renamed *Gustave Zédé* (ex-*Sirene*), she was 48.5m (159.1ft) long and displaced 270 tonnes (266 tons); armament was a single 45cm (18in) tube for launching two Whitehead torpedoes. The hull was made of bronze to avoid corrosion, and like the *Gymnote*, accumulator batteries provided current for an electric motor, sufficient to take the boat submerged from Toulon to Marseilles.

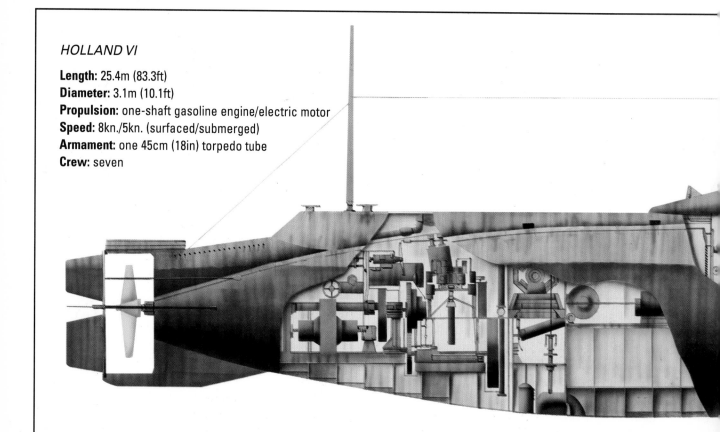

HOLLAND VI

Length: 25.4m (83.3ft)
Diameter: 3.1m (10.1ft)
Propulsion: one-shaft gasoline engine/electric motor
Speed: 8kn./5kn. (surfaced/submerged)
Armament: one 45cm (18in) torpedo tube
Crew: seven

Below: John Holland was so disillusioned by the arguments over the *Plunger* that he offered to build a submarine at his own expense. The result was the *Holland*.

Above: The Royal Navy's 'A' class were British-designed improvements over the Holland boats of 1901. Vickers' expertise enabled the Navy to avoid reliance on US patents.

The French Ministry of Marine was enthusiastic about the new weapon, and in 1892 ordered a larger boat to Romazotti's design, named the *Morse*. Her 36.5m (119.7ft) hull was also made of bronze and incorporated the best features of the *Gymnote* and *Gustave Zédé*. Although successful she had the misfortune to be overshadowed by a new French development.

In 1896 the new Minister of War, Edouard Lockroy, announced an open competition to design and build a 203-tonne (200-ton) submarine with a range of 185.2km (100 miles) on the surface and 18.52km (10 miles) submerged. Out of 29 designs submitted the winner was Maxime Laubeuf with the *Narval*, using a novel dual propulsion system: a steam reciprocating engine on the surface and an electric motor for submerged running. Even more significant was the use of oil fuel, stowed in tanks between the main 'pressure' hull and the light external hull. Although accumulator batteries were provided, they could be recharged by a generator driven by the steam engine.

The *Narval*, ordered in 1899 and delivered in 1900, attracted worldwide attention, but she had several drawbacks. It took at least 15 minutes to shut down the

Above: Once the decision was made to buy *Holland*-type submarines for the Royal Navy, progress was swift. *Holland No.1* was launched by Vickers on 2 October 1901.

boiler before diving, and the complex apparatus for folding down the stubby funnel and closing the hatch was a source of potential weakness. Henceforward the small battery-driven submarines would be known as sousmarins, whereas the dual-propulsion type would be known as submersibles. Ironically, in modern terminology the reverse is true: diesel-electric boats are often described as submersibles, in contrast to nuclear-powered 'true submarines'. The *Narval* was, in principle, a submersible torpedo boat, carrying her four 45cm (18in) torpedoes slung externally in Drzewiecki drop-collars.

The French Navy was so impressed by the *Narval's* trials that four 'Sirene' class of slightly enlarged design were ordered in 1899–1900, even before the prototype's trials could be evaluated. (The Fashoda Incident had just brought France to the brink of war with Great Britain, and France urgently needed an 'equaliser'.) In 1899, another design was prepared by M Maugas, the four 'Farfadet' class, bringing the French total of submarines to 12 by 1905.

THE US NAVY – EXPERIMENTAL DESIGNS

The US Navy had never totally lost interest in submarines, and had issued requests for bids to build experimental boats in 1888 and again in 1889. Holland's design won against rival proposals, but at the first request the shipyard selected refused to guarantee performance, and a year later the cash-starved navy was forced to divert funds elsewhere.

A third competition held in 1893 was won by Holland again, and funds finally became available two years later. In 1895 the Navy Department awarded a $150,000 contract to the John P Holland Torpedo Boat Company, which was subcontracted to the Columbian Iron Works in Baltimore the following year.

Launched as the *Plunger* (chronologically *Holland V*) in 1897, the new boat ought to have been the final vindication of Holland's persistence, but the navy had set wildly unrealistic performance targets. To combine a surface speed of 15 knots with an armament of two torpedo tubes in a 40m (131.2ft) hull, Holland was forced to adopt triple-screw steam propulsion as well as electric drive. During basin trials in 1898 the steam plant created a temperature of 137°F at only two-thirds power. Clearly this turkey would never fly, and Holland washed his hands of the project, refunding the $93,000 advanced by the Navy Department. It was, however, only a pawn in a bigger game and Holland's political friends were able to persuade the navy to reallocate the money to a smaller private venture to be built by the Crescent Shipyard at Elizabethport, New Jersey. This was the *Holland* (*Holland VI*), displacing 65 tonnes (64 tons), just under 25.4m (83.3ft) in length, and driven by a gasoline engine and electric motor. Her trials were a

great success, and the navy agreed to buy her at the same price it had been willing to pay for the *Plunger*.

Although the American press praised the little *Holland* as a 'Monster War Fish' and other lurid titles, she was a very primitive craft. She had a submerged range of about 74km (40 miles) at a very nominal five knots, and a diving depth of no more than 25m (82.02ft), but had no periscope and so was virtually blind underwater. On the surface her 45hp Otto engine gave her a theoretical endurance of 2778km (1500 miles), but with no accommodation for the crew she could barely manage a few hours at sea. The US Navy was sufficiently impressed, however, to order six more of a slightly enlarged design in 1900, the 'Adder' or 'A' class.

Holland's only serious competitor was a fellow American, Simon Lake. His *Argonaut Junior* was a wooden-hulled prototype built in 1894 as a private venture. The *Argonaut First*, 17m (55.8ft) long and displacing 60 tonnes (59 tons), was built alongside the *Plunger* and launched in August 1897. She proved successful, and had several features which would later prove to be sound. These included a double hull and a more effective means of maintaining a level trim than the *Holland* boats. However, Lake had a poor appreciation of the warlike possibilities of submarines and was more interested in running on the seabed to assist salvage divers and to recover objects. He did include a torpedo tube in his next boat, the *Protector* (1902), but retained the concept of wheels for running on the seabed to allow divers to cut submarine cables in time of war. Although the *Protector* was bought by the Imperial Russian Navy in 1911, Lake's emphasis on these features irked the US Navy to the point that he was soon left behind by Holland, who gave the navy what it asked for. With hindsight it is obvious that the ideal solution would have been a collaboration between the two brilliant designers, for Lake had much to contribute.

THE ROYAL NAVY REPLIES

The sudden proliferation of submarines alarmed the Royal Navy, which decided that it ought to investigate the new technology, but not in such a way as to alarm the public. As early as February 1899 the First Lord of the Admiralty was 'not at present prepared to make a statement' in reply to parliamentary questions about the French developments. Another question in the House of Commons a year later was answered by an attempt at lofty disdain: 'Submarines are a weapon for Maritime Powers on the defensive', and in any case, the Admiralty 'knew all about them'. The debate was not helped by a speech made by Admiral Sir Arthur Wilson VC, who denounced submarines as 'underhand, unfair and damned un-English' and recommended that in wartime submarine crews should be hanged as pirates.

That irascible comment has been quoted out of context to suggest that the Admiralty had closed its mind on the subject of submarines, but in fact an internal study had already begun. The Director of Naval Construction pointed out correctly that his department had no expertise in the field, and recommended the purchase of a Holland design from the Electric Boat Company (successor to the Holland Torpedo Boat Co). A contract was signed in

Below: Although the five *Hollands* performed satisfactorily, the Admiralty wanted to develop its own expertise, especially avoiding reliance on the Electric Boat Co.

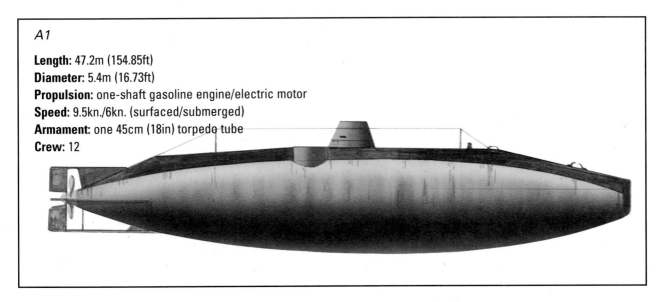

A1

Length: 47.2m (154.85ft)
Diameter: 5.4m (16.73ft)
Propulsion: one-shaft gasoline engine/electric motor
Speed: 9.5kn./6kn. (surfaced/submerged)
Armament: one 45cm (18in) torpedo tube
Crew: 12

December 1900 to allow Messrs Vickers Sons & Maxim to build five submarines at Barrow-in-Furness. The specifications differed little from the US Navy's 'Adder' class: a maximum surface speed of eight knots (seven knots in moderate weather), a 463km (250 mile) radius at full speed, seven knots submerged and a 46.3km (25 mile) radius (three and a half hours). Submerged endurance was to be 15 miles, and maximum diving depth was set at 47m (154.1ft). But these figures proved optimistic: at full power the batteries only lasted for one hour and the maximum recorded depth was 37m (20 fathoms). Nevertheless, the Royal Navy took these problems in its stride. They were simply numbered Submarines 1–5, but were always known as *Holland No.1* etc.

Acquiring the *Hollands* was a bold stroke, for it avoided considerable risk, and as soon as HM *Submarine No.1* was launched on 2 October 1901 the Submarine Service became a reality, with a ready supply of volunteers. Fort Blockhouse at Portsmouth was to be the base (later to become HMS *Dolphin*). An 'A' class of 13 boats was ordered in 1901, using Vickers' expertise to eliminate reliance on US patents. They were followed by the 10 'B' class in 1903, giving the Royal Navy a comfortable margin of 28 submarines.

THE RUSSIAN NAVY

The Imperial Russian Navy had shown no reluctance to experiment with submarines, ever since the 18th Century, so the initiatives at the beginning of the century are hardly surprising. A very small boat, the 23.6m (77.4ft) *Pyotr Koshka* ('Peter the Kitten') was launched at Kronstadt in 1902, but her endurance was limited to 16.66km (nine miles) at full speed and her externally carried torpedoes were unreliable. The *Delfin*, launched in 1903, was an improvement, but she was sunk by accident in the River Neva at the Baltic Shipyard the following year. With war against Japan in the Far East looming there was no time for a leisurely approach, and in 1904 the Russians bought the *Fulton* from the Electric Boat Co. and the *Protector* from the Lake Submarine Co. Renamed *Som* and *Ossetr* respectively, both were sent on the Trans-Siberian Railway to Vladivostok, but neither achieved anything. The experimental *Forelle* was also bought from Krupp's Germania shipyard in Kiel in 1904 and shipped to the Far East by rail, but played no part in the war. More Lake and Holland designs were bought, while indigenous designs were developed by Professor Bubnov. Three were also bought from Krupp's Germania yard in 1904, the 'Karp' class boosting the nominal strength of the Baltic Fleet to 17 boats by 1908.

LATE DEVELOPERS – THE GERMANS

Readers who assume that Germany led the rest of the world in developing the submarine will be surprised by the Imperial German Navy's tardiness in entering the race. The role of the little *Forelle* was critical. Originally laid down as a private venture, using a design prepared by the Spaniard, Raimondo Lorenzo d'Equevilley Montjustin, she impressed the naval

Below: The Royal Navy's 'Holland' class was very similar to the US Navy's 'Adder' class. *Holland No.1* sank in 1913, but after raising resides in the Submarine Museum, Gosport.

HOLLAND No.1

Length: 16.3m (53.47ft)
Diameter: 3.1m (10.17ft)
Propulsion: one-shaft gasoline
Speed: 8kn./7kn. (surfaced/submerged)
Armament: one 45cm (18in) torpedo tube
Crew: 12

officers at her trials in 1903. d'Equevilley was an engineer who had worked for Maxime Laubeuf, and he had tried unsuccessfully to offer the French Ministry of Marine his own design in 1901. When the French learned he had turned to Krupp they concluded that he had stolen the design of the latest French submarine, the *Aigrette*, but Krupp's designers always denied this.

As we have already seen, the *Forelle* was sold to Russia in 1904, but d'Equevilley was given another chance, this time with the 'Karp' class. These impressive submarines had a double hull and were driven on the surface by a Körting kerosene engine. Clearly d'Equevilley and the Krupp team recognised the weakest point of the Holland designs – their petrol engines. The Körting might send clouds of dense white smoke into the air, but there was no toxic explosive vapour to permeate every compartment of the hull, waiting for a single electrical spark to create havoc. The German Navy Ministry was quick to order a very similar boat from the Germania yard, *U.1*, which is still displayed in the Deutsches Museum in Munich. In March 1906, six months before *U.1* completed her trials successfully, the Kaiserliche Werft in Danzig (Gdansk) was awarded a contract to build the *U.2* to an official design. She was 50 per cent larger and had four 45cm (18in) torpedo tubes (two forward and two aft) as against only one bow tube in *U.1*.

Above: As a submarine pioneer the French Navy had its fair share of disasters. When the *Farfadet* sank off Toulon in 1901, a Royal Navy salvage team helped raise her.

Submarine technology was moving rapidly from the age of experiments to a process of evolution, but one major hurdle remained. Only the French Navy seemed willing to follow the path of the reciprocating steam engine for surface propulsion, but the other submarine operators were well aware of the limitations of Holland's petrol-engined designs. The Germans solved the problem with the Körting kerosene-fuelled engine, and the British had installed an experimental 'heavy oil' engine in *A.13*, not a true diesel but still relying on compression for ignition.

The most advanced engine available was the diesel. Although invented by a German, Dr Rudolf Diesel, the Imperial German Navy took a long time to adopt it for U-boats. It was left to the French to install diesel engines in the *Aigrette* and *Cicogne* in 1904, followed by the British 'D' class in 1908, the Russian *Minoga* in 1909 and the US Navy's *Turbot* ('G' class) and the German Navy's 'U.19' class in 1912–13.

The diesel was the last major advance in submarine design before the submarine made its debut in World War I. It cured the worst problems of power : weight ratio and safety, and despite many other giant strides in submarine technology it is still in use today, even in nuclear submarines as a 'get-you-home' system.

Baptism of Fire

By the outbreak of World War I in August 1914 a large number of submarines had been built, but navies were to find that the new weapon had its limitations. However, despite their weaknesses, they soon challenged the supremacy of the surface warship, and came close to winning the war for Germany.

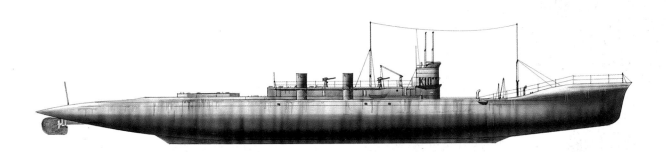

At the outbreak of war in August 1914, nearly 300 submarines were in service, with another 80 or more on order or planned. Despite their late start the British and the Germans had overtaken the French and Americans, having 77 and 29 boats respectively. Although many navies had bought foreign designs and had then built improved versions, the leading submarine builders were still to be found in Great Britain, France, Germany, Italy and the United States.

Despite endless speculation about the role of submarines, navies had little or no idea of how to use them. All the belligerents and the neutral countries regarded themselves as bound by the provisions of International Law and the clauses in the 1899 and

Left: A gun crew prepares to fire the deck gun of a Royal Navy 'E' class submarine. In World War I deck guns proliferated as an easy means of attacking 'soft' targets.

1907 Hague Conventions governing the conduct of war at sea. With no experience of submarine warfare since the American Civil War it was assumed that a submarine was like any other warship, ie, it was not permitted to fire on a neutral merchant ship. The submarine was supposed to board the merchant ship, examine her papers and ascertain that she was trading with the enemy. If her cargo manifest indicated that she was carrying contraband the submarine was to put a prize crew on board and send her to a friendly port for adjudication. The submarine could, of course, sink the ship with a torpedo or gunfire, but the captain and crew would lose the prize money awarded from the proceeds of the sale of the cargo. The survivors were to be put into lifeboats, but if the weather was too rough or the distance to land too great, the submarine was to treat the crew as shipwrecked mariners and take them on board.

The Prize Regulations, which enshrined these principles, favoured the large mercantile fleets of Great Britain and France, but took no account of the peculiar nature of the submarine. Stopping a merchantman required the submarine to surface, thereby forfeiting her principal advantage of secrecy. The crew of a submarine was too small to provide prize crews and there was certainly no room for prisoners, so a submarine adhering to the Prize Regulations would either be exposed to counter-attacks from enemy warships or be limited to intercepting one or two merchant ships at most.

The Imperial German Navy had taken to heart the views of American naval historian Captain Mahan, who had noted that the vastness of the British merchant fleet was simultaneously her strength and her weakness. Much thought had been given to the use of warships against commerce, but the use of submarines was at first very timid. On 20 October 1914, Kapitänleutnant (K/Lt) Feldkirchner's *U.17* made history by stopping the steamer *Glitra* off Norway and sinking her after sending the crew away in lifeboats.

Most naval officers, however, saw the enemy's warships as the true targets for submarines, a belief which seemed borne out by events. As soon as war broke out both the British and the Germans sent submarines to observe enemy movements, while in the Mediterranean the French and Austrians did the same.

In the North Sea both sides were disappointed. Although the Royal Navy's submarines provided sufficient information to permit a raid on German light forces in the Heligoland Bight, they found that torpedoes tended to run underneath their targets. The German U-boats found that extended cruising put great strain on machinery, and many broke down. *U.15* was repairing such a breakdown when she was spotted by the light cruiser HMS *Birmingham*, which rammed her and sent her to the bottom. Both sides found that surface warships tended to shoot first and ask questions later; several submarines were attacked by their own side. Mines accounted for a U-boat as early as 12 August, but as yet minefields were comparatively few and covered only small areas.

BRITISH COMPLACENCY SHATTERED

The complacency of the Royal Navy was shattered very early on during the war. On 22 September a single U-boat, *U.9*, under the command of K/Lt Otto Weddigen, torpedoed three 12,192-tonne (12,000-ton) armoured cruisers, HMS *Aboukir*, HMS *Cressy* and HMS *Hogue*, off the Dutch coast. Weddigen's feat

Right: The cramped interior of the German *U.155*, formerly the cargo submarine *Deutschland*, after the Armistice (probably in French hands).

Below: Seven large German submarines were converted in 1916–17 to carry high-value cargoes from the United States. Those that survived were subsequently armed.

DEUTSCHLAND

Length: 100.75m (330.54ft)
Diameter: 13.4m (43.96ft)
Propulsion: two-shaft diesel engines/electric motors
Speed: 12.4kn./5.2kn. (surface/submerged)
Armament: nil as built
Crew: 56

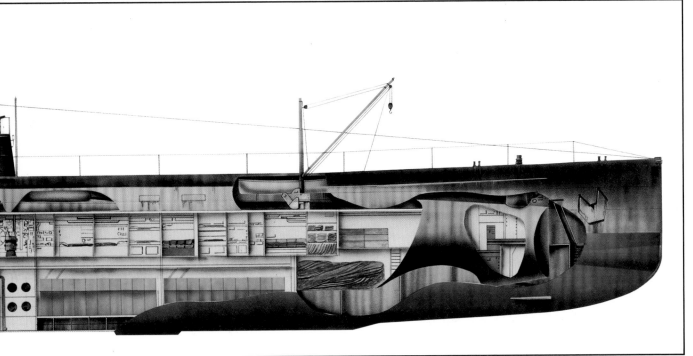

was helped by the British cruisers' initial assumption that they had blundered into a minefield, but the loss of three major warships and many of their large crews was a bitter blow to British pride. Weddigen's reputation as the first U-boat 'ace' was confirmed when three weeks later he torpedoed another old cruiser, HMS *Hawke*, off Aberdeen. *U.9*'s victim was lying hove to in the process of transferring mail, and there were similar examples of ships' captains seemingly oblivious to the new threat, piping 'Hands to Bathe' or steaming slowly in waters known to be patrolled by submarines.

Above: U-boats alongside a depot ship in Kiel in 1913: (left to right) *U.12, U.7, U.10* and *U.6*. The Germany Navy's U-boat designs steadily improved during the war.

The Royal Navy's main force, the Grand Fleet, had moved its base from Rosyth on the Firth of Forth to Scapa Flow, a huge natural anchorage in the Orkneys. But the Grand Fleet was still undefended, and a sudden 'U-boat scare' was enough to paralyse it. Although no U-boat ever penetrated the Flow during the war, the panic-stricken Navy moved the Grand Fleet to a succession of temporary anchorages on the

U.9

Length: 80.94m (265.55ft)
Diameter: 9.3m (30.5ft)
Propulsion: two-shaft kerosene engines/electric motors
Speed: 14kn./8kn. (surfaced/submerged)
Armament: four 45cm (18in) torpedo tubes (two bow, two stern)
Crew: 29

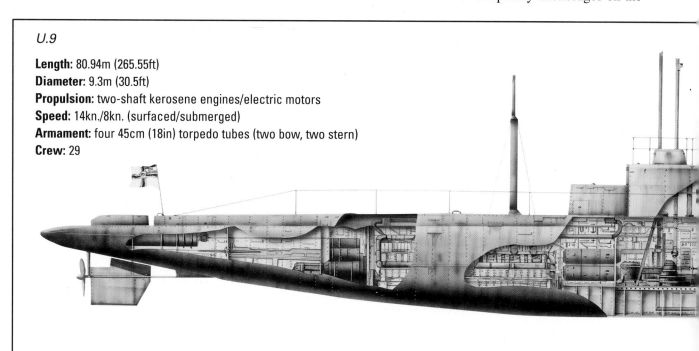

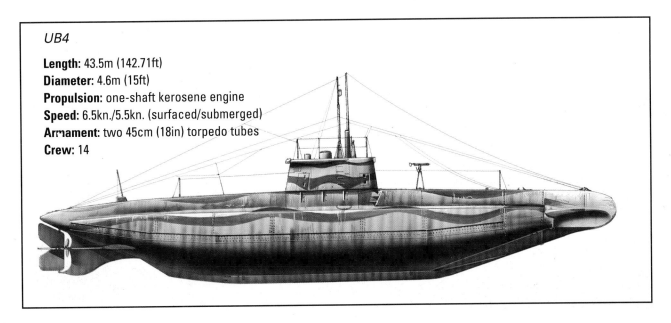

UB4

Length: 43.5m (142.71ft)
Diameter: 4.6m (15ft)
Propulsion: one-shaft kerosene engine
Speed: 6.5kn./5.5kn. (surfaced/submerged)
Armament: two 45cm (18in) torpedo tubes
Crew: 14

Above: One of the small German 'UB' type coastal submarines put into production after the outbreak of war. They were small enough to be transported by rail.

west coast of Scotland until nets, blockships, guns and searchlights could be put in place around the Flow. It was the first strategic victory for submarines, forcing an entire fleet to abandon its chosen area of operations. Such a move might have given the High Seas Fleet a decisive victory, but there were too few U-boats, and none reliable enough to be risked so far from their bases. In any case, the chance was missed,

for the Grand Fleet returned to Scapa Flow – and refastened its grip on the High Seas Fleet.

U-BOATS

The strength of the U-boats stood at 29 at the outbreak of war, with *U.30* still incomplete and 20 more under construction. This modest total underlines High Command's obsession with the surface fleet, and its conviction that the role of U-boats was merely to inflict attrition on the Grand Fleet as a prelude to a fleet action. However, the U-boats proved to be well designed for the task, and the latest design was put into

Below: Under K/Lt Otto Weddigen, *U.9* made history in September 1914 by sinking the British cruisers *Aboukir*, *Cressy* and *Hogue* off Holland.

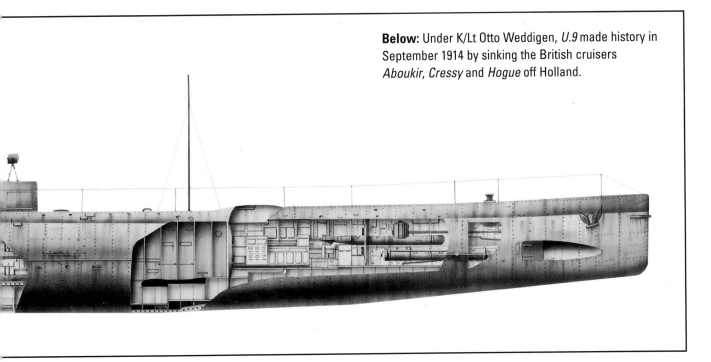

quantity production. At the same time a small coastal design, the 'UB' type, was put into production, along with a specialised 'UC' minelaying type. The 'UB' series was very small and because of the shortage of diesel engines, the hated Körting kerosene engine was used. The Russians had pioneered the minelaying submarine with the *Krab* in 1908, but the Germans adopted a different system, with vertical chutes inside the forward part of the pressure hull. The mine and sinker were dropped from the chute, and a soluble plug

Above: *U.53* arrived uninvited at Newport, Rhode Island, in October 1916. She left without provoking an international incident, but the US Government was angered by the U-boat's audacity, not overawed as Germany hoped.

Below: Until convoys were introduced in 1917, U-boats were able to destroy large numbers of targets by gunfire from their deck guns. This saved torpedoes for bigger targets, thereby extending substantially the time that the U-boat could spend on patrol.

U.31

Length: 65.4m (214.56ft)
Diameter: 6.4m (21ft)
Propulsion: two-shaft diesel engines/electric motors
Speed: 16.7kn./9.7kn. (surfaced/submerged)
Armament: four 50cm (19.68in) torpedo tubes, one 88mm gun
Crew: 35

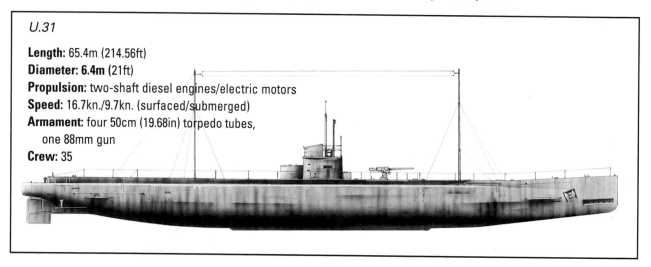

delayed arming of the mine until the UC-boat was clear – in theory. In July 1915 the British found that *UC.2* had managed to blow herself up in her own minefield. She was raised and a British version of the system was adopted for some of her 'E' class.

The sea-going U-boats became known generically as the 'Mittel-U' type, and as the war against commerce progressed a number of modifications were incorporated. The armament of four 50cm (20in) torpedo tubes (two bow and two stern) remained standard for a surprisingly long time. But the deck gun proved so useful for sinking merchant ships that it was increased from a 8.8cm (3.4in) calibre to 10.5cm (4.1in). This led to the concept of the 'cruiser U-boat', armed with two 15cm (5.9in) guns, despite pleas from officers at sea for more torpedoes. By the end of the war the armament of the 'Mittel-U' type had increased to four 50cm (19.7in) tubes forward and two aft, and the 'U.117' class was given external stowage for 24 torpedoes. The little 'UB' design was successfully developed into a very effective seagoing type, the 'UB III' series which compared well with larger pre-1914 boats. The 'UCs' underwent a similar evolution, culminating in the 'UC III' series in 1918, with an endurance of 14,816km (8000 miles) and 14 mines.

BREACHES OF INTERNATIONAL LAW

The sinking of the SS *Glitra* did much to change the Naval Staff's perception of the value of a commerce war, particularly because all the commerce-raiding cruisers had been sunk or captured by 1915. The Grand Fleet had not behaved as the German planners had hoped (by refusing to risk a close blockade of German harbours), and when it left harbour on one of its frequent sweeps it was screened by destroyers. One such foray cost Weddigen his life in the new *U.29*, when his periscope was sighted by a lookout aboard the battleship HMS *Dreadnought* on 18 March 1915 in the Pentland Firth. In response to a rapid helm order the 18,289-tonne (18,000-ton) ship wheeled out of line and sliced the luckless U-boat in half. The ruthlessness with which the British enforced the blockade also weakened any scruples entertained by the German Naval Staff about breaches of International Law. For example, all foodstuffs were declared contraband by the Allies, on the grounds that the German government had commandeered all food supplies.

An unrestricted war against Allied shipping carried with it a risk of losing the propaganda war. The torpedoing of the Belgian refugee ship *Amiral Ganteaume* in October 1914 was just such an incident, labelled an atrocity by Allied newspapers. Knowing how little a U-boat commander could actually see through a periscope, it is likely that *U.24* mistook the *Amiral Ganteaume* for a troopship. With only a distorted image and only a few seconds for a torpedo shot, the U-boat captain was supposed to count the number of people on deck, guns, and even where the guns were mounted. Forward-mounted guns indicated offensive armament, whereas aft-mounted guns counted as defensive armament under the Prize Regulations. When *U.20* first sighted the liner *Lusitania* in April 1915, K/Lt Schwieger mistook her four funnels and smoke for a flotilla of destroyers! Only when he returned to Germany did he learn the name of the ship he had sunk. Despite the opinions of conspiracy theorists, even if the German Naval Staff had an inventory of munitions carried in the hold of the *Lusitania*, *U.20* could never have identified an individual ship with such precision.

Even without flouting their self-imposed restrictions, the German Navy's U-boats were inflicting painful losses on the Allies: 32,513.6 tonnes (32,000 tons) of British and 16,155 tonnes (15,900 tons) of French and neutral shipping sunk in January 1915 alone. By March the monthly total had risen to 81,995 tonnes (80,700 tons), and by May the figure topped 187,969 tonnes (185,000 tons). Neutral opinion, particularly in the United States, was outraged. The

Below: A German U-boat engages a target during the campaign in the Atlantic. One unfortunate consequence of deck guns was to reduce underwater performance.

Above: *U.35* off Cattaro, the Austro-Hungarian Navy's base in the Adriatic, in April 1917. The availability of a major base in this area increased U-boat effectiveness.

insatiable demands of the Allied war economies had opened a huge new market to replace that cut off by the blockade. Neutral opinion was inflamed by lurid tales of the rape of Belgium; the deaths of American citizens at sea added fuel to the fire.

Ignoring the uproar, Germany announced on 4 February 1915 the existence of a War Zone around the British Isles, in which British and French merchant ships would be sunk without warning. The declaration added ominously that it would not always be possible to avoid attacks on neutral ships. In other words, U-boats could 'sink at sight' unless they saw a neutral flag. If the neutral maritime nations could have forbidden trade with the Allies the German gamble might have paid off, but the tight British blockade meant that a refusal to trade with the Allies would mean virtual bankruptcy for most shipping companies. It was the same fact of maritime life which had brought down Napoleon's Continental System, but in 1915 nobody seemed to pay much attention to the lessons of history.

AN UNRESTRICTED CAMPAIGN

The German Army's conquest of a large part of Belgium gave a vital fillip to the U-boat war. When

Below: The four 'Andrea Provana' class submarines were built in 1915–18 by FIAT–San Giorgio at La Spezia. Ironically, they missed the war for which they were built.

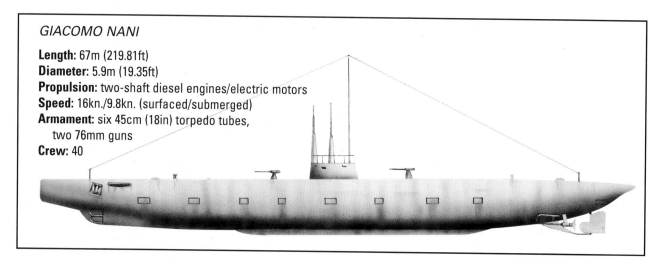

GIACOMO NANI

Length: 67m (219.81ft)
Diameter: 5.9m (19.35ft)
Propulsion: two-shaft diesel engines/electric motors
Speed: 16kn./9.8kn. (surfaced/submerged)
Armament: six 45cm (18in) torpedo tubes, two 76mm guns
Crew: 40

the front stabilised after the Battle of the Marne in August 1914, the German right flank rested on the Flanders coast at Nieuport. The Navy soon established a base complex at Ostend, with submarines and light surface forces based there and at Zeebrugge. U-boats were based at the inland port of Bruges and reached the open sea by canals to Ostend and Zeebrugge, allowing them to spend more time at sea in the Western Approaches and the Bristol and St George's Channels. British minefields and net barriers in the Dover Straits were not effective as U-boats soon learned to make the passage on the surface at night. To allow the British to continue believing in the efficacy of their Dover Straits anti-submarine barriers, U-boats based in Germany would 'show themselves' occasionally to Royal Navy patrols.

The Allies' answer to the unrestricted campaign was to increase the number of patrol vessels by impressing every available warship and hired commercial craft. A new type of utility warship, the 'Flower' class sloop, was taken off minesweeping duties and used instead to hunt for submarines. The Auxiliary Patrol was formed out of the large number of steam yachts, trawlers and drifters which were no longer performing any useful function. Armed with light guns, the patrol was sent on fruitless hunts for

U-boats around the British Isles. In fact the sea is so large that the U-boats merely had to wait near a busy shipping route until an unescorted vessel came along. If a patrol vessel appeared it was usually possible to submerge without being sighted.

THE *LUSITANIA*

Nothing illustrates the ease with which U-boats could sink shipping than the tragedy of the liner *Lusitania*. Most British transatlantic liners had been taken over in 1914 for conversion to armed merchant cruisers or troopships, but with government approval the *Lusitania* was permitted to resume a limited passenger service between Liverpool and New York. The reasons for this were subtle and complex. First, the giant liner was a visible reassurance to the American public that it was still 'business as usual', and that Britain's position as Mistress of the Seas was not under serious threat. Second, the Germans had put up an ingenious answer to the British blockade, claiming that their U-boats had instituted a counter-blockade of the British Isles. If this claim had been

Below: A 'UB I' type coastal submarine on the surface, with most of her crew on the conning tower and casing. The framework on the bow is a submarine net cutter.

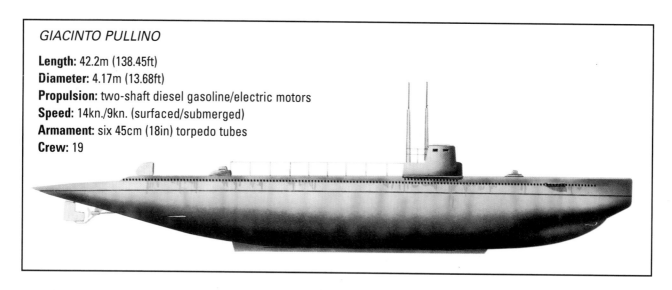

GIACINTO PULLINO

Length: 42.2m (138.45ft)
Diameter: 4.17m (13.68ft)
Propulsion: two-shaft diesel gasoline/electric motors
Speed: 14kn./9kn. (surfaced/submerged)
Armament: six 45cm (18in) torpedo tubes
Crew: 19

upheld in an international tribunal the Germans would have been within their rights to sink any ship trying to reach the British Isles. However, to be upheld it would have to be proven to be 'effective', and by maintaining a scheduled service to and from New York the British Government was quietly keeping its options open. There was also still some hope that the Germans would never dare to sink a large passenger ship, for fear of alienating the US Government.

Much has been made of the fact that the *Lusitania* was carrying explosives, and indeed her manifest reveals that she was carrying 37.59 tonnes (37 tons) of small-arms ammunition and fuse nosecaps. It has even been claimed that she was armed, despite the lack of any evidence to show that she underwent conversion to an armed merchant cruiser. True, she had been taken up in August 1914 for that purpose, but she had proved such a glutton for coal that she was struck off the list a month later and returned to her owners. No other auxiliary cruiser carried passengers as well as a cruiser-armament, for the simple reason that the passenger accommodation was needed for conversion to naval use, and the unpredictable movements of a liner under naval control would have taken bookings down to zero very quickly. Nor did passengers and explosives mix; the passenger accommodation was a potential firetrap, and a liner had too little cargo space to make such a conversion worthwhile. The 37.59 tonnes (37 tons) of rifle ammunition and fuses formed the most inert type of munitions, almost impossible to detonate by a distant explosion. Whatever anyone thought, or knew, the *Lusitania* was carrying when she lay in New York is irrelevant, because the information about her future position could not be relayed to any U-boat on the other side of the Atlantic. When in due

Above: Completed in December 1913, in July 1916 the *Giacinto Pullino* was beached on Galiola Island and seized by the Austrians. She later sank while being towed.

course the *Lusitania* was torpedoed by *U.20* off the Old Head of Kinsale on 7 May 1915, it suited both sides to claim that the sinking was planned. The Germans claimed that as they knew about the small cargo of munitions, *U.20* was entitled to sink her, while the British claimed it was a Hun plot to sink innocent ships. The truth is that K/Lt Schwieger's log shows beyond doubt that his encounter with the *Lusitania* was unplanned. He chose to patrol off the Old Head of Kinsale because it was a convenient landfall for ships arriving in British waters. When he saw the four funnels belching coal smoke he thought he was looking at a flotilla of destroyers in line ahead, and only when the target turned did he see she was a liner. As his orders stated that a number of troopships were expected from Canada, he made the reasonable assumption that this was a legitimate target. Any idea that he could have counted positions of guns is ridiculous, and recent photographs of the wreck show no guns. The ship's rapid sinking after what was reported by Schwieger as a second explosion is explained by modern chemists as a probable spontaneous combustion of air and coal dust – a phenomenon only vaguely understood in 1915.

Among the dead were 159 Americans, and this time the US Government's protests were stronger than before. A Note from Washington to Berlin demanded that U-boats must refrain from attacking passenger ships. The Germans did not handle the diplomacy well, maintaining that they had warned potential passengers of the danger. This merely fuelled suspicions that the

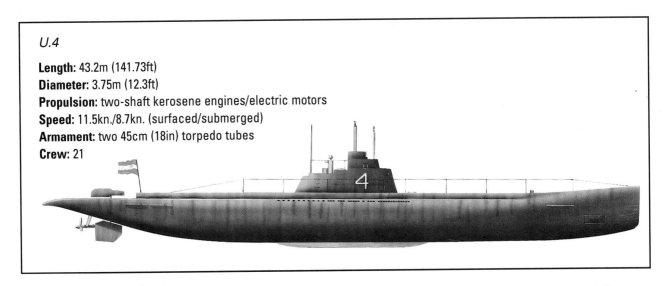

U.4

Length: 43.2m (141.73ft)
Diameter: 3.75m (12.3ft)
Propulsion: two-shaft kerosene engines/electric motors
Speed: 11.5kn./8.7kn. (surfaced/submerged)
Armament: two 45cm (18in) torpedo tubes
Crew: 21

ship had been torpedoed deliberately. The British did nothing to damp down these rumours, although if anyone had thought the 'conspiracy theory' through they would have concluded that German agents must be in control of the Cunard Steamship Company or even in command of the ship, if such a perfect interception was to be achieved.

ALLIES RESPOND TO LOSSES

The *Lusitania* incident was a milestone in the history of the submarine. The ship was not the first to go down with American citizens aboard, but she was the one which was remembered. The outcry forced the Germans to abandon the unrestricted campaign, but in 1916 losses began to climb again, until the monthly total exceeded 508,025 tonnes (500,000 tons).

The losses were fast approaching a catastrophic level:

1914	tonnes	tons
3 ships totalling	2997	(2950)
1915		
640 ships totalling	1,208,115	(1,189,031)
1916		
1301 ships totalling	2,229,640	(2,194,420)
1944	*3,440,752*	*(3,386,401)*

Sadly a large number of these losses were the small sailing ships such as fruit-carrying schooners, which still plied the Atlantic in large numbers. They were particularly vulnerable to attack by gunfire. The figures do not include the warships sunk.

The Allies responded with more auxiliary patrol vessels, arming of merchant ships and the famous 'Q-ships'. These were decoys, armed and manned by naval personnel, which cruised in the U-boats'

Above: Two boats, numbered III and IV (renumbered *U.3* and *U.4* in 1915), were built in Germany in 1907–09. *U.3* was sunk in 1915, but *U.4* survived the war.

hunting grounds. As the majority of attacks were made on the surface with gunfire, to conserve torpedoes, it was possible for the Q-ship to sink the U-boat before being sunk herself. The combination of armed merchant ships and decoys led the U-boat commanders to attack on sight, and a few enterprising officers tried to leave no witnesses by machine-gunning the survivors, a policy known as *spürlos versenkt*.

An impression that the U-boats were the only effective submarines would be very misleading. In the North Sea the British submarines were active, the new 'E' class proving to be well designed. On 13 September 1914 *E.9* sank the old light cruiser SMS *Hela* off Heligoland, and repeated her success by sinking the destroyer *S.115* on 6 October. In January 1915 *U.17* was torpedoed in error by *U.22*, a tragedy to be repeated many times in two world wars when navigation errors put friendly submarines in the wrong place. In July 1915 the destroyer *V.188* was torpedoed by *E.15*, and two months later *U.6* was sunk by *E.16*. In addition some of the old 'C' class were used to stop German attacks on the fishing fleets. Requisitioned naval trawlers were modified to allow them to tow a submerged 'C' boat, with a telephone link to pass information on the range and bearing of the U-boat. The trawler *Taranaki* and *C.24* sank *U.40* off Aberdeen in June 1915 and a month later the *Princess Louise* and *C.27* sank *U.23* off Fair Isle. By a stupid error the survivors of the two U-boats were allowed to mix with civilians waiting to be repatriated to Germany, so the 'trawler trap' was soon

known to the U-boat command, but it had the desired effect of reducing attacks on the fishing fleet. But for the most part Royal Navy submarines were confined to reconnaissance, hoping to spot German surface ships on their rare sorties.

THE BRITISH IN RUSSIA

If North Sea operations seemed humdrum, there was soon pressure to help the Russians by sending submarines to the Baltic. In October 1914, *E.1* and *E.9* left for the Kattegat, arriving at Libau (modern Lipaja) just as the Russian Army was evacuating the port in the face of advancing German forces. But a new base was quickly established at Lapvik on the Gulf of Finland, where the minor repairs needed after such a long voyage could be done. The two boats had already made their mark, Lieutenant Commander Laurence in *E.1* making an unsuccessful attack on the cruiser SMS *Viktoria Luise* in the Kattegat, and Lieutenant Commander Max Horton in *E.9* sinking the destroyer *S.120* off Kiel. What shook the German Navy was the fact that Horton's attack was carried out in the winter ice, when submarines were supposed to be confined to harbour. The aggressive Horton had, however, ascertained that he could operate as long as the inlet valves did not freeze, and demanded a Russian icebreaker to clear a passage out of Lapvik to the open sea.

Below: A Royal Navy 'E' class submarine lifting her bows in a heavy swell. The housed periscope suggests she is about to dive, although men are still on the conning tower.

The depredations of the two boats put new heart into the Russians, whose nominally huge force was largely useless because the diesels and electric motors were on order from Germany. The Lake-designed *Drakon* carried out more patrols than any other Russian boat, and the rest of them might have achieved much more, but for the timidity of the High Command. The British boats were not there to sink warships, but primarily to attack the iron ore traffic from Sweden to Germany, although this did not inhibit *E.8* from torpedoing the big armoured cruiser SMS *Prinz Adalbert* off Libau in November 1914. Nevertheless, the British boats proved so effective that the German High Command convinced itself that a whole flotilla was operating in what was nicknamed 'Horton's Sea' by the *Kaiserlichemarine*, and time was wasted looking for an imaginary depot ship in the western Baltic. The Admiralty finally decided that reinforcements were needed, and in August 1915 four more 'E' class were sent out. One was lost, *E.13*, which ran aground off the Danish coast and was destroyed by gunfire from German destroyers, but *E.8*, *E.18* and *E.19* arrived safely at Lapvik. In addition four of the old 'C' class were sent as deck-cargo to Arkhangelsk, and then taken by canal barge and rail to Lapvik.

By October 1915, nine British submarines were operational, and, as the efficiency of the Russian boats improved, German losses rose alarmingly the following year. But Russian morale was collapsing as the land campaign continued to go against her, and the

Above: The side-by-side arrangement of torpedo tubes in the forward torpedo room of an 'E' class submarine. Experience was to prove the need for heavier bow salvoes.

efficiency of the Lapvik base declined rapidly after the 'February Revolution' of March 1917 when the Kerensky government came to power. The October Revolution signalled the end, and when the Bolsheviks signed the Treaty of Brest-Litovsk early in 1918 they agreed to German demands to surrender the British submarines, now based at Helsingfors (Helsinki). This was not going to be tolerated by the Admiralty, and on 8 April 1918 an icebreaker manned by some of the few remaining 'friendly' Russians led the surviving seven boats out to deep water. There they were scuttled by their crews, who were then evacuated through north Russia. They had performed outstanding work, dislocating the iron traffic and diverting German naval forces which could have been used elsewhere.

THE MEDITERRANEAN

Royal Navy submarines were also sent to the Mediterranean, to work with the French against the Austro-Hungarian Navy. The Germans had also sent U-boats to work with their allies, and a joint base was

set up at Cattaro (Kotor). Italy joined the Allies in May 1915, but declared war only on the Austro-Hungarian Empire. *U.21,* under K/Lt Otto Hersing was sent from Cattaro to Constantinople to set up a half-flotilla with five UB-boats. He made the risky passage of the Dardanelles safely, but only four of the smaller boats made it.

The Anglo-French attack on the Dardanelles in the spring of 1915 ushered in a new submarine campaign. The Allies quickly learned that they could not push surface ships past the guns and minefields in the Narrows, and so they turned to submarines. However, the risks were very obvious. Not only were there five rows of mines, but the four to five knot current caused severe navigation problems. The only submarines available were three old British 'B' class and the French *Brumaire* and *Circé.* As early as 1 December 1914, *B.11* had achieved an exciting passage through the Narrows, and her crew's determination was rewarded by the sinking of the old Turkish coast defence ship *Messudieh.*

When more modern submarines arrived, another attempt was made to get submarines through the Straits and into the Sea of Marmora beyond. The first two attempts were a failure: *E.15* ran aground off Kephez Point and the French *Saphir* ran aground off Nagara. The Australian boat *AE.2* had the honour of being the first to reach the Sea of Marmora, but she was soon sunk by a Turkish torpedo boat. *E.14* followed the next day, but the French *Joule* was lost to a mine, making the loss rate a total of four submarines for only one success. Thereafter things improved, and soon *E.14* was joined by another six British boats and the French *Turquoise.* Although the *Turquoise* was an early casualty, the British submarines caused havoc, slowing the shipment of troops and munitions to the Turkish defenders at Gallipoli. Their most notable success was the old battleship *Hairredin Barbarossa* (formerly the German *Kurfürst Friedrich Wilhelm*), torpedoed by *E.11* in August 1915, but landing parties sabotaged railway lines as well. The campaign only finished when the British and the Anzacs evacuated the Gallipoli Peninsula in January 1916.

The German and Austro-Hungarian U-boats were very effective in the Mediterranean. On 25 May 1915 Hersing in *U.21* sighted the old battleship HMS *Triumph* firing at Turkish trenches at Gaba Tepe. He waited two hours to get the perfect shot, a single torpedo which sent his victim down. Two days later he sighted the battleship HMS *Majestic* at anchor off Cape Helles but surrounded by colliers and patrol

vessels. Once again his patience was rewarded, and when a gap opened he sank the old ship with a single shot. Faced with such a threat the Royal Navy had no option but to withdraw the battleships and cruisers to Mudros, leaving the troops with only light fire support until specialised bombarding ships could be sent out from England. It was an outstanding success by any standards.

French submarines operated mainly in the Mediterranean, and although they scored a number of successes they were not as effective as the British and German boats. The designs were ingenious but not all the ideas were practical, the multiplicity of types making logistic support a nightmare. The modern boat *Curie* tried to enter Pola (Pula) on 20 December 1914, but was caught in the nets and sunk by gunfire. The Austrians raised the wreck and repaired it, renaming her *U.14.* When she was returned to the French Navy after the war, she provided many lessons and remained in service until 1928.

GERMANY TRIES ITS HAND

The *Kaiserliche und Königliche (KuK) Kriegsmarine* had only seven submarines in 1914, all distinguished by roman numerals. These include two Lake boats, two Germania type and three Holland type. The last of these, *XII,* had been built as a private venture by Whitehead at Fiume, but was seized at the outbreak of war. She should have been numbered *VII,* but that number had been allocated to one of a series of five large Germania boats ordered in 1913. These were never delivered, becoming *U.66* to *U.70* in the German Navy. To compensate for this the Austrians were given five small 'UB' boats, numbered *X* (ex-*UB.1*), *XI* (ex-*UB.15*), and *XV* to *XVII* (German-style Arabic U-numerals were not adopted until October that year). When Italy declared war on Austria on 23 May 1915 from Germany to Cattaro the newly delivered *X* and *XI* operated with their German crews in the Adriatic, sinking the Italian submarine *Medusa* and the torpedo boat *No.5PN* in June 1915. In August the French destroyer *Bisson* rammed and sank *III* in the Otranto Straits, and *U.5* (ex-*V*) was mined off Pola in 1915. *U.16* suffered a bizarre fate; she torpedoed the destroyer *Nembo* in May 1916 off Valona, but was destroyed when her victim's depth-charges blew up.

Just as both sides came to realise their respective potential in the water, a new threat appeared: the aircraft. Ironically, the clear waters of the Mediterranean, as seen from the air, were dangerous to submarines, and the French *Foucault* was the first

victim, bombed in September 1916 off Cattaro by two Austrian seaplanes. Technically the British *B.10* was the first, being destroyed at Venice in August 1916, but she was in dock at the time.

Back in the North Sea, the Germans were still trying to circumvent the Allied blockade. In June 1916 a new large 'commercial' submarine, the *Deutschland*, left Kiel bound for the United States with a cargo of mail, chemical dyes and gemstones. The propaganda value was immense, and crowds flocked to see the submarine at Baltimore. She sailed for Germany late in July, laden with copper, nickel, silver and zinc. It was hoped to repeat the performance in September 1916, but this time it backfired. The *Bremen* disappeared somewhere off the Orkneys (almost certainly mined), leaving her escort, *U.53*, to head for Newport, Rhode Island alone. Her command, K/Lt Hans Rose, milked the occasion for all it was worth, chatting to embarrassed US Navy officers while their superiors pestered Washington for instructions. As a neutral country, the United States was not supposed to allow a belligerent nation's submarines to abuse its territorial waters. However, Rose's cockiness led him to start attacking shipping off the Nantucket lightship; the head of the U-boat Arm, Commodore Hermann Bauer, had told him that 'bold action' would silence the anti-German party in America and result in the ban on unrestricted warfare being lifted.

In fact the opposite happened, as the US government became even more worried about German intentions, while the US Navy started to take the submarine threat very seriously. The 'commercial' submarine was never going to carry enough cargo to justify such trips, and the *Deutschland* and her sisters were armed with two 50cm (19.7in) torpedo tubes, two 15cm (5.9in) guns and two 88mm (3.4in) guns. Known as 'cruiser-submarines', they were numbered *U.151* to *U.157*. The decision to upgun all the larger U-boats was prompted by the Allies' decision to arm merchantmen, but the provision of medium-calibre guns was a waste of time. If submarines met any

Below: The officers and men of HM Submarine *E.11* pose for a photograph at Mudros after their success in sinking the Turkish battleship *Hairredin Barbarossa* in August 1915.

target they could not handle with guns in the 7.62–10.16cm (3–4in) range, something bigger would not save them. Gunnery from the low deck of a submarine was poor at the best of times, with no fire control system to calculate range. It was no better from the poop of a tramp steamer – and defensive guns probably did more good for morale.

ROYAL NAVY – EXPERIMENTAL SUCCESSES

Although the Royal Navy's 'E' class was proving ideal for its North Sea and Mediterranean operations (57 were built by 1916), the pre-war submariners were in the mood for experiments to see if they could do better than relying on Vickers. Scott's was asked to build three boats to an Italian Laurenti design, the 'S' class, while Armstrong's was asked to build four to a French Schneider-Laubeuf design, the 'W' class. As a sop to Vickers, the firm was allowed to submit its own 'V' design. In practice, the large-scale experiment proved inconclusive, as there was no chance in wartime for adequate comparative trials. The four 'V' class were retained but the 'S' and 'W' class were transferred to the Italian Navy, which it was felt would be better able to understand their 'foreign' equipment.

Two other experimental ideas were initiated by the Royal Navy about this time, a big ocean-going 20-knot boat intended to match the German U-boats, and a steam-driven design. The first, HMS *Nautilus* (later numbered *N.1*), had many problems and never went to sea, but valuable lessons were learned. She ended her troubled days as a generating station in Chatham Dockyard. The second, HMS *Swordfish*, was given a single geared steam turbine because the designers could not guarantee the required 20 knots with avail-

able diesels. She was only a qualified success, and after a year she was rebuilt as the surface patrol vessel *S.1*.

Admiral Sir John Jellicoe, the Commander-in-Chief of the Grand Fleet was obsessed with the belief that the High Seas Fleet were going to sea accompanied by fast (22-knot) U-boats, and kept nagging for an equivalent. To meet this requirement a new 'fleet' submarine, the 'J' type was ordered in January 1915. No diesel engine of the required power existed, so the 8-cylinder engine in the 'E' class was redesigned with 12 cylinders, and the new design was given three, each driving its own shaft. Even that was not enough to get within two knots of the Grand Fleet's speed of 21 knots – proof that the 1912 requirement was unrealistic. They were, however, well armed with four 45cm (18in) bow torpedo-tubes, two beam tubes and 12 torpedoes. Their long-range radio sets allowed them to send sighting reports from the Heligoland Bight, without going through a 'repeating ship'.

In April 1915 Vickers sent Commodore Hall, head of the Submarine Branch, an outline for a submarine driven by a combination of steam turbines and a diesel engine. A 1913 proposal was unearthed, and when the best features of both were combined, it seemed to solve the problem of the 'fleet submarine' better than anything yet seen. A similar armament to the 'J' class was adopted, and two boilers provided steam for two geared steam turbines, developing 10,000 hp for a surface speed of 24 knots. Instead of driving a centre shaft with the diesel, as in the Vickers proposal, it was

Below: The 57 'E' class boats were the workhorses of the Royal Navy's submarine force in 1914-18, though nearly half were lost during the course of the war.

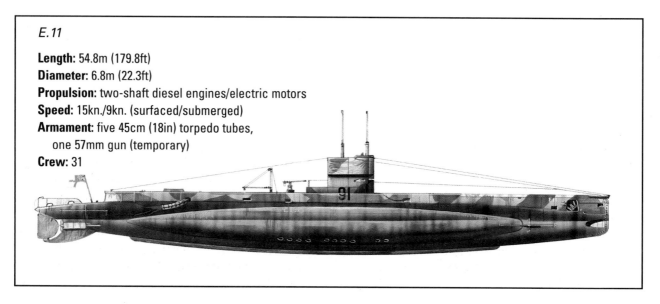

E.11

Length: 54.8m (179.8ft)
Diameter: 6.8m (22.3ft)
Propulsion: two-shaft diesel engines/electric motors
Speed: 15kn./9kn. (surfaced/submerged)
Armament: five 45cm (18in) torpedo tubes,
one 57mm gun (temporary)
Crew: 31

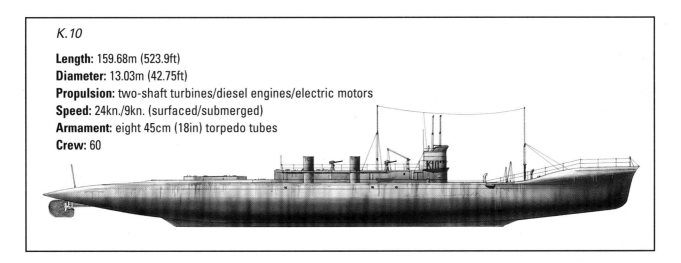

K.10

Length: 159.68m (523.9ft)
Diameter: 13.03m (42.75ft)
Propulsion: two-shaft turbines/diesel engines/electric motors
Speed: 24kn./9kn. (surfaced/submerged)
Armament: eight 45cm (18in) torpedo tubes
Crew: 60

linked to a 700 hp dynamo to supply power to the two electric motors. This was the first diesel-electric plant in a British submarine. Because the submarines were intended to spend a lot of time on the surface the armament was strengthened by a pair of twin 45cm (18in) revolving tubes in the long superstructure. The gun armament included two 10.16cm (4in) guns and a 7.62cm (3in) anti-aircraft gun, another first. This was the infamous 'K' class, which earned a reputation for bad luck and disaster.

THE INFAMOUS 'K' CLASS

The 'K' class problems took two forms. The boats were very large and complex, and had a comparatively shallow crush-depth (50 per cent more than their length). In theory the steam plant would be shut down and the electric motors would be clutched in before diving, but in practice there was sufficient steam in the boilers to send the boat down at her maximum speed of close to 24 knots. At that speed the control surfaces could not always bring her under control fast enough, and there was a very real danger that the boat would plunge below the safe diving-depth. There were, to quote a contemporary officer, 'too many damned holes'. There was a constant risk of a small blockage preventing the mushroom-topped ventilators and funnel wells from jamming slightly open as the boat dived. But the worst problem of all was the operational concept itself. The boats were intended to operate in proximity to surface warships, which could easily fail to spot them at night or in fog, or mistake them for a U-boat. The long hull was not easy to manoeuvre, and avoiding action would be difficult. Another contemporary submariner described them as 'handling like a destroyer, but having the bridge facilities of a picket boat'. The field of view from the low conning tower put a 'K' boat at a great

Above: The notorious British 'K' class was built to meet a demand for submarines fast enough to keep up with the battle fleet. This meant steam turbines and oil-fired boilers.

disadvantage. All that notwithstanding, the 17 'K' class were an extraordinary achievement, just 15 years after *Holland No.1*.

The reputation for bad luck was well deserved. While *K.13* (a number asking for trouble!) was running trials in the Gareloch at the end of January 1917 she sank when her engine-room ventilators failed to shut properly. Loss of life was heavy but she was eventually raised, repaired and recommissioned as *K.22*. Despite some hair-raising incidents, only *K.1* was lost off the Danish coast after colliding with *K.4*, and they were successfully integrated into the Grand Fleet. In January 1918, a major sweep by the capital ships based in the Firth of Forth was planned, with two flotillas of 'K'-boats to go ahead of the leading battlecruiser squadron.

On the night of 31 January a jammed helm caused *K.22* to sheer out of line and collide with *K.14*. The battle cruisers following failed to notice (strict radio silence was in force), and HMS *Inflexible* inflicted severe damage on *K.22* as she passed. The flotilla leader HMS *Ithuriel* and the remaining three boats of the 13th Submarine Flotilla turned back, and became mixed up with the light cruiser HMS *Fearless* and the four boats of the 12th Flotilla. In the ensuing confusion the *Fearless* rammed and sank *K.17*, and later *K.6* cut the hapless *K.4* in half. To add to the horror the 5th Battle Squadron and its escorting destroyers ploughed through the area, killing a large number of the survivors of *K.17* (there were none from *K.4*).

The so-called 'Battle of May Island' was not caused by any design fault of the 'K' class; the disaster was

caused entirely by the flawed concept of mixing surface warships and submarines. Yet, this example has consistently been used by critics to belabour the Royal Navy for its alleged incompetence in submarine design. It is only fair to point out that in 1918 the German *Marineamt* drew up plans for large steam-driven U-boats for the same reason – the lack of sufficiently powerful diesels.

THE SUBMARINE MONITOR

The Royal Navy still had a few tricks up its sleeve. In response to a request from Commodore Hall for a 'submarine monitor' with a heavy-calibre gun, four 'M' class were ordered in February 1916. Although frequently described as converted 'K' hulls, they were a totally new design, armed with an old 30.48cm (12in) 35 calibre gun. The mounting was unique, elevating from -10 degrees to +20 degrees and training through 15 degrees. A special method of firing, the 'dip-chick', was developed, with the submarine lying at periscope depth and only the muzzle of the gun above the surface. Four were ordered but only *M.1* to *M.3* were completed in 1918.

The 'R' design was revolutionary, a submarine designed specifically to hunt other submarines. It incorporated many modern features, notably a highly manoeuvrable whale-shaped streamlined hull reminiscent of the modern 'teardrop', a heavy bow salvo of six torpedo tubes, a big array of passive hydrophones in the bow, and high underwater speed (15 knots). Ten 'Rs' were completed and one attacked a U-boat in October 1918 but the torpedo failed to explode. It was a soundly conceived design, but the sensors were not yet available to make the 'Rs' an operational success.

GERMANY REVIVES

Although Germany had been forced by American diplomatic pressure to stop unrestricted submarine warfare in 1915, the High Command continued to chafe under the restrictions. After the fearful losses at Verdun and the failure to defeat the Grand Fleet at the Battle of Jutland in May 1916, Germany was no longer certain of victory. The Navy supported the Army in its clamour to remove the shackles on the U-boats, although the diplomatists kept reminding them of the risk of bringing America into the war. The High Command finally won the argument, and in February 1917 the Kaiser gave official

approval to the renewal of unrestricted warfare. The Navy was now getting the U-boats ordered after the outbreak of war, and the daily average of boats at sea from no more than 10 in mid-1915 to 30 by the end of 1916, and by mid-1917 it would be 40. It was accepted that America was eventually coming into the war, but the admirals and generals argued that the destruction of shipping on an unprecedented scale would force the British to sue for peace. With the Atlantic dominated by U-boats the Americans could not intervene, even if they wanted to, and without American and British support France could be dealt with at leisure.

Right: The 'swan bow' of HM Submarine *K-12* hid a quick-blowing tank, added after completion, to bring up the bows faster when surfacing. The raised bridge aided visibility.

The first results justified all the optimism. Within weeks losses rocketed to 812,840 tonnes (800,00 tons) a month. British and French countermeasures were totally inadequate, and one in four of the ships entering the War Zone was certain to be sunk. When the United States finally entered the war in April 1917 Admiral William S Sims of the US Navy went to London to meet the First Sea Lord, now Sir John Jellicoe. Sims was shocked to learn that the war was near to being lost, and food stocks for only six weeks remained. The Admiralty no longer knew which way to turn. The supreme example of U-boat success was Lothar Arnauld de la Periére, whose various U-boats sank the largest total of all:

	tonnes	tons
1915		
35 ships totalling	90,62	89,192
1916		
122 ships totalling	267,050	262,832
1917		
62 ships totalling	173,411	170,672
1918		
5 ships totalling	13,416	13,204
	544,500	***535,900***

Above: HM Submarine *M.2*, one of three armed with a 12in gun for shore bombardment and surface attack. After the war she was converted to launch a small floatplane.

In 1917, the U-boats sank the appalling total of 3170 ships, a total of 6,033,328 tonnes (5,938,023 tons), and in 1918 they sank a further 1280 ships totalling 2,666,398 tonnes (2,624,278 tons). These bald statistics conceal the slaughter of seamen, both Allied and neutral, who were drowned, burned or died of exposure. At this distance in time it is difficult to understand how such a position was allowed to develop. The British war leaders in particular must bear some of the blame for trying to pretend that it was 'business as usual', and the general optimism exemplified by the First Lord of the Admiralty, Winston Churchill, that it would be a short war. Virtually all construction of merchant ships had stopped by the end of 1914, to allow yards to build warships. No ocean salvage organisation existed, so crippled vessels were not towed to port, and in any case the workers in repair yards had been allowed to enlist in the Army. Damaged merchantmen were laid up, or in some documented cases, sunk by escorting warships. There was a blind refusal to see shipping as a war asset; every ship which arrived safely was potentially capable of carrying another cargo, but a ship sunk meant the loss of future carrying capacity.

In the summer of 1916 the Admiralty finally realised that the pool of available shipping was drying up. A salvage organisation was created and orders were placed for a new generation of standard merchant ships. Yards were created in Canada and Japan to build these ships, although most were not ready until the worst of the crisis was over.

CONVOY

One more countermeasure had not been adopted, the convoying of ships. Convoy (the grouping of merchant ships under the protection of warships) was a very old means of protecting ships and their cargoes; during the Middle Ages wine ships had crossed the Channel from Bordeaux to England in convoy, and it had been the standard method of commerce protection in the Napoleonic Wars. But the Admiralty persisted in using incorrect statistics to 'prove' that convoy could not work because there were not enough escorts. Only French insistence forced the British to convoy colliers taking coal to France from February 1917. In April that year, at the worst moment of the U-boat campaign, the collier convoys were suffering 0.19 per cent losses, as against 25 per cent everywhere else. This was proof enough for the influential officers in the Trade Division to lobby for the general

adoption of convoy. The Admiralty fought back with all the conviction of the truly bigoted, and it seemed that the war would be lost before a decision could be made.

The argument over who can take the credit for introducing convoy is hard to resolve. The Prime Minister, Lloyd George, was only too happy to claim it, but it was almost certainly urged on him by the Cabinet Secretary, Maurice Hankey, who had already been won over by the Trade Division. With all the cunning at his command Hankey persuaded Lloyd George to overrule the Admiralty Board, and amid dire warnings of disaster the first ocean convoy sailed

at the end of April. To everyone's amazement the loss rate fell from 25 per cent to 0.24 per cent at the end of May. By November 84,000 passages had been made in convoy, and only 257 ships had been sunk.

For the U-boats it was the end of easy pickings. Smoke on the horizon now portended the arrival of a formation of ships escorted by destroyers and patrol vessels and even airships. All U-boat commanders' reminiscences harp on the fact that targets disappeared, and gun attacks on the surface were no longer safe. Each submarine had only one shot at the convoy, reducing its chances of hitting anything, and that shot would bring immediate retaliation with depth charges or bombs.

Later in the year it was at last possible to take the offensive against the U-boats. A new horned mine, modelled on the German one, was now available in large numbers, and nightly minelaying runs into enemy waters blocked exit routes from the U-boat bases. Cryptanalysis enabled U-boats to be ambushed, hydrophones could detect submerged targets, and the depth charge enabled them to be attacked below the surface.

When the war ended in November 1918 the German Navy was forced to surrender all sea-going U-boats in Allied ports. Some 360 had been built, and 400 more lay incomplete or had been cancelled as the German war economy collapsed under the competing demands of the Army. They had sunk 11,176,550 tonnes (more than 11 million tons) of shipping and damaged 7,620,375 tonnes (7.5 million tons) more, but the cost was the loss of 178 U-boats and 5364 officers and ratings, nearly 40 per cent of the total.

Below: The British 'M' class boats were conventional in layout, apart from their large guns. These could be fired from periscope, using a bead-sight on the muzzle.

M.1

Length: 90.14m (295.73ft)
Diameter: 7.5m (24.6ft)
Propulsion: two-shaft diesel engines/electric motors
Speed: 15kn./9.5kn. (surfaced/submerged)
Armament: four 45cm (18in) torpedo tubes,
   one 12in gun, one 76mm gun
Crew: 64

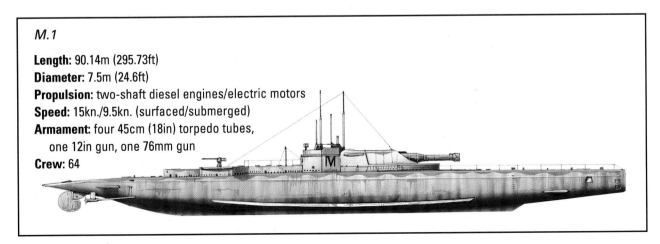

CHAPTER THREE

Submarines in World War II

Submarine design made great strides between the two world wars, and in 1939–45 showed once again that submarines could inflict immense damage on enemy shipping. The German offensive in the Atlantic was finally defeated, but the Japanese never found an answer to the American campaign which destroyed her maritime power.

The conditions of the Treaty of Versailles included a total ban on submarines for the truncated *Reichsmarine* which replaced the old Imperial Navy after the abdication of the Kaiser. The giant armada of U-boats disappeared in a very short time, scrapped except for a handful permitted to be used for experimental purposes by the victorious Allies. But Germany never intended to accept the harsh conditions of the Treaty, and very quickly the team of

Left: A Type VIIC U-boat returns to her base on the Atlantic coast of France during the war. This type was the workhorse of the Battle of the Atlantic.

designers at Krupp's Germania yard, led by Dr Hans Techel, moved to Holland to establish a clandestine Submarine Development Bureau behind the facade of the *Ingenieurskantoor voor Scheepsbouw* (Shipbuilding and Engineering Office). Its aim was to keep abreast of submarine technology and to develop its own designs for the *Reichsmarine*'s future needs. At the same time a torpedo research programme was set up in Sweden, again with secret funding from the Navy. Neither the Netherlands nor Sweden, ardent upholders of neutrality, have ever deigned to explain their dubious roles in permitting such a flagrant evasion of an international disarmament treaty.

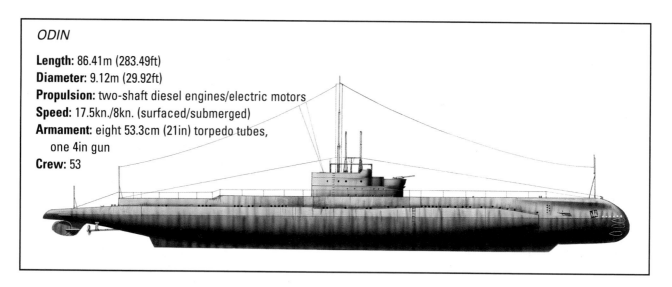

ODIN

Length: 86.41m (283.49ft)
Diameter: 9.12m (29.92ft)
Propulsion: two-shaft diesel engines/electric motors
Speed: 17.5kn./8kn. (surfaced/submerged)
Armament: eight 53.3cm (21in) torpedo tubes,
one 4in gun
Crew: 53

Above: The British 'O' class boats incorporated lessons learned during World War I, but their external fuel tanks made them vulnerable to attack.

Most navies were unduly impressed by the U-cruisers, and set about designing their own in the postwar years. Predictably, none of the designs justified their cost, but the British *X.1* (two twin 13.5cm- [5.2in-] gun mountings), the American *Argonaut* (*V.4*), *Narwhal* (*V.5*) and *Nautilus* (*V.6*) with two single 15.2cm (6in) each, and the French *Surcouf* (a twin 20.3cm [8in] turret) set new records. The Royal Navy found the *X.1* a great disappointment, and looked at more interesting uses for its three 'M' class. *M.2* was converted to launch and recover a small Parnall Peto floatplane, while *M.3* became a minelayer.

NEW DEVELOPMENTS

Floatplanes were very attractive for scouting in distant waters, and the idea had been tried during the recent war by the British and the Germans. The US Navy fitted *S.1* with a tubular hangar on the after casing, with a tiny folding floatplane, but the Imperial Japanese Navy found the idea irresistible. After building a number of cruiser-submarines in the 1920s, the Type J1M prototype *I.5* was built with a seaplane and catapult. The tubular hangar was part of the conning tower, split to accommodate the wings in one section and the fuselage and floats in the other. With 44,448km (24,000 miles) range at 10 knots, 111.12km (60 miles) submerged at three knots, a diving depth of 90m (295.2ft) and stores for 60 days, she was the prototype for *I.6* (Type J2) and the 'I.9' and 'I.15' classes (Types A1 and B1). Armament was heavy: six 53.3cm (21in) tubes and 20 torpedoes, and two 13.8cm (5.43in) guns.

As a weak naval power Japan had shown an interest in submarines as early as 1906, and the experience of World War I impressed on her the importance of building a large fleet. Her broad strategic aim was to use submarines with the main fleet, to inflict attrition on the enemy (Great Britain and the United States) before offering battle with the surface fleet on favourable terms. The latest Royal Navy boats, the 'L' class built in 1916–24, inspired the Kaidai and L3 types, which ran to over 30 boats with 'RO' numbers. They formed the bulk of the submarine force in the 1930s, complementing the big *Junsen* type ocean-going boats.

The French opposed any limit on submarine numbers at the Washington Naval Disarmament Conference in 1921–2. Some influential senior officers led by Admiral Daveluy, tried to prove that submarines could replace surface fleets entirely. With the support of the influential chairman of the Naval Estimates Committee, M de Kerguezec, they proposed a fleet of 200 to 250 submarines. The French Navy's rebuttal of this doctrine makes interesting reading. The alleged cheapness of the submarine was illusory, and ton-for-ton they were as expensive as battleships. They also required a large number of highly skilled people to build, operate and maintain them. Furthermore, their complexity gave them a shorter operational life – a submarine with worn-out systems is unsafe to dive.

After the first hectic round of post-war experimentation most navies realised that the medium-sized boat, displacing 762–1524 tonnes (750–1500 tons) on the surface, was best suited to their needs. Coastal submarines were also needed, to operate in the shallow waters denied bigger boats. By 1931, submarine-operating navies had 26 large boats in service, 188 medium-sized, 233 small types and 123 under construction.

The Soviet Union's Red Fleet had saved a few Tsarist boats: six in the Baltic, 18 in the Black Sea, eight in the Caspian and one in the Arctic. The first new design, the 'D' or 'Dekabrist' class, was ordered in 1927 to an Italian design. The British *L.55*, sunk in the Baltic during the Intervention War in 1919, was raised in 1928 and the lessons learned were incorporated into a new 'L' or 'Leninets' class. The Germans also provided technical support for the 'S' or 'Stalinets' class. It bears a strong resemblance to the contemporary Type VIIA design, but German sources say that the wartime 'UB III' design was the basis. Other designs ranged from the 'K' type cruiser-submarines to the 'M' type coastal boats, small enough to be transported by rail.

The Scandinavian navies had collective experience as far back as 1904, when Sweden launched the 172.7-tonne (170-ton) *Hajen*. The Royal Netherlands Navy had also been in the submarine business, with O-numbered *Onterzeeboote* for home service and K-numbered *Kolonien* boats with roman numerals for the East Indies. With the help of the Germania team in Rotterdam it is not surprising that Dutch shipyards did well in export markets during the inter-war period.

The Royal Navy made one small but important change – replacing numbers with names, and arranging them in alphabetical series, starting with 'O'. After *X.1* the first new design was the 'Oberon' or 'O' class, running through to the 'T' class by 1939. The exceptions were three high-speed fleet boats, the 'River' class, and the 'Porpoise' class minelayers, named after marine mammals. British designs were exported to Chile, Estonia, Portugal, Turkey and Yugoslavia. Two classes were selected for mass-production in wartime, the proven sea-going 'S' class and the bigger ocean-going 'T' class, but shortly before the war a small coastal design, the 'U' class, was designed to replace the ageing 'H' class for training. Fortunately a decision to give them no armament was rescinded, and they too were built in large numbers during the war.

When Adolf Hitler became Germany's new Chancellor in 1933 the Navy had already prepared its

Below: An unusual assortment of Royal Navy submarines late in the war. The are (left to right): an early 'S' class, a 'U' or 'V' class, P-614, HMS *Upright* and HMS *Unison*.

Above: HMS *Unrivalled*, one of the improved 'U' class. They could be distinguished from the pre-war boats by their 'shark' bow. Designed for training, they also saw combat.

masterplan to defeat the Versailles Treaty ban on U-boats. The Naval Staff had prepared plans for five types: a sea-going design of 508–762 tonnes (500–750 tons) based on the 'UB III' of 1917, an ocean-going minelayer, a 1524-tonne (1500-ton) U-cruiser, a 254-tonne (250-ton) coastal boat and a 508-tonne (500-ton) coastal minelayer. The minelayer types and the cruiser-type were not built, but the others were selected as the basis for future construction. By November 1934 material bought clandes-tinely from Holland, Finland and Spain had been assembled, sufficient for 10 Type II coastal boats. With Hitler's approval progress was rapid, and 24 were under construction before the end of 1935. To the British Admiralty, who had worked so hard to prevent this happening, it was a severe blow.

ADMIRALTY TRIES TO CONTAIN HITLER

As Germany's new naval programmes could not be stopped, the alternative was to contain and direct it, an aim achieved by the Anglo-German Naval Treaty of 1936, which agreed to parity in submarines but only one-third of Royal Navy strength in surface ships. This agreement has been denounced as appeasement

---

TYPE XXI

Length: 76.7m (251.64ft)
Diameter: 6.6m (21.65ft)
Propulsion: two-shaft diesel engines/electric motors
Speed: 15.6kn./17.2kn. (surfaced/submerged)
Armament: six 53.3cm (21in) torpedo tubes, two 20mm guns
Crew: 57

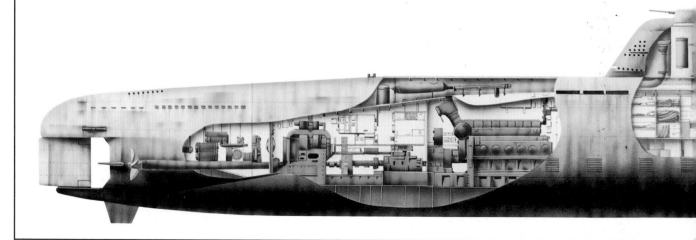

at the time (and since), but it controlled German expansion. One important benefit was the choice of the nominally 508-tonne (500-ton) Type VII design (actually 762 tonnes [750 tons]), in order to make best use of the total tonnage available. As the war progressed it became clear that the design was too small for Atlantic work, but by then it was too late to redesign the hull.

In August 1939 the *Führer der Uboote*, Admiral Karl Dönitz, had under his command 65 U-boats, including 32 Type II coastal boats, 12 Type I and Type IX ocean-going boats and 21 sea-going Type VIIs,

although 10 were still fitting out. When war broke out the following month a total of 21 boats were at sea. This time Hitler was determined to avoid antagonising American opinion, and the U-boats were ordered to observe the Prize Regulations to the letter. These were enshrined in an international protocol signed several years earlier, in a well-meant attempt to 'humanise' submarine warfare. The Admiralty did not

Below: HMS *Thrasher* returning to base in October 1945. She reflects all the wartime changes to the 'T' class: bulbous bow, aft-firing tubes and 20mm cannon.

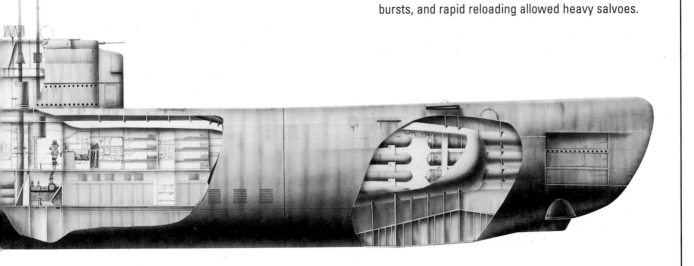

Below: By increasing battery capacity, the Type XXI boats achieved high underwater speed for short bursts, and rapid reloading allowed heavy salvoes.

believe for a moment that the Regulations would work in practice, and had already warned Merchant Navy captains to expect a 'sink-at-sight' policy. Nor was there any debate about the value of convoy, although the lack of escorts prevented 'close' escort all the way across the Atlantic. When K/Lt Julius Lemp in *U.30* mistook the liner *Athenia* for a troopship on the day after the outbreak of war and torpedoed her, he was threatened with a court martial. But the Propaganda Ministry took a hand, seizing *U.30*'s log and accusing Winston Churchill and the Admiralty of sinking the liner themselves to incriminate Germany.

Even when operating under the Prize Regulations the U-boats managed to sink 114 ships totalling 427,915 tonnes (421,156 tons), up to the end of December 1939. The regulations were held to expire at the end of September 1939, allowing U-boats to attack any ship sailing without lights off the British or French coasts. On 4 October this exemption was extended out to 15 degrees West, followed by permission two weeks later to sink any ship identified as

hostile. The last prohibition, on attacking liners, was removed on 17 December, and unrestricted warfare was back.

UNRESTRICTED WARFARE

The most spectacular successes of the first weeks were, however, against warships. On 12 September *U.29* sank the aircraft carrier HMS *Courageous*, which was on patrol in the South Western Approaches. The hunt took two hours, but K/Lt Schuhart's patience was rewarded when the carrier turned into wind to recover her aircraft. Even so, she might have escaped had not two of the escorting destroyers been detached to help a sinking merchant ship. Two days later the new carrier HMS *Ark Royal* was narrowly missed by a salvo of torpedoes from *U.39* passing astern. This time the U-boat paid the price, and the carrier's escorts sank *U.39* with depth-charges. The Admiralty hurriedly decided that big carriers were too valuable to be risked in pointless anti-submarine patrols.

Exactly a month later K/Lt Günther Prien in *U.47* achieved a brilliant success by penetrating Scapa Flow and sinking the old battleship HMS *Royal Oak* at anchor. Aerial reconnaissance had revealed that 20 years of fierce currents and winter gales had shifted

Below: *U.47* and her crew in festive mood. The VIIA lacked the prominent wind deflector around the top of the conning tower and other refinements.

Above: The massive anti-aircraft armament (one 37mm and two twin 20mm guns) and radar 'mattress' give some idea of the wartime additions to the Type VII boats.

the blockships scuttled in Kirk Sound in World War I. The U-boat Command gave permission for Prien to try to find a way into the vast natural harbour. Only two attempts had been made by U-boats in 1914–18 to penetrate the Flow's defences, and both had ended disastrously, so Prien had no illusions about the risks. On the night of 13 October 1939 *U.47* just scraped past the rusting blockships and their mooring chains, grounding once. The Flow was virtually empty because the Home Fleet was at sea, but lookouts spotted the *Royal Oak* to the north. Because one bow tube was faulty the U-boat could only fire a salvo of three torpedoes, and Prien was mortified to hear only a small explosion, possibly a hit on the anchor chain or a partial 'dud'. Prien turned the boat around to try a shot with the single stern tube, but that missed too, so he withdrew to allow the bow tubes to be reloaded. This time all three ran true and detonated under the *Royal Oak*'s keel. Thirteen minutes later the 23-year-old veteran rolled over and sank, taking with her 833 officers and ratings.

The U-boat Arm was wildly elated, and Prien and his crew were showered with honours. Even if the *Royal Oak* was an elderly unit, her loss had shown the

Admiralty that Scapa Flow was no longer secure. The Home Fleet was forced to move to a temporary base in Loch Ewe on the west coast of Scotland until Scapa Flow could be made safe once more, repeating the experience of the Grand Fleet in 1914. But the *Kriegsmarine* was no more able to exploit the Fleet's temporary absence than its predecessors had been, and the opportunity never recurred.

ESCORT VESSELS

The Admiralty had drawn up elaborate plans for the immediate convoying of merchant ships. All that was lacking was sufficient escorts, and to make up for the shortage 'close escort' was only provided out to 15 degrees West. In coastal waters constant air patrols were effective in keeping sinkings down, and when the new 'Flower' class corvettes began to enter service in the spring of 1940 they too operated effectively in coastal waters. To avoid this lethal concentration of resources the U-boats were forced to move further west, and to cope with this, close escort was provided to 17 degrees West from July 1940, and then to 19 degrees West three months later.

On the other side of the Atlantic the Royal Canadian Navy had to extend its convoy limit from 56 degrees to 53 degrees West. This left the 'Black Gap' in mid-Atlantic, in which merchant ships had neither air cover nor escorts. All that saved the Atlantic convoys from

Above: K/Lt Otto Kretschmer and his crew of *U.99* at Kiel in May 1940 – a 'happy time' for the U-boats.

Below: The death of *U.118* at the hands of aircraft from the carrier USS *Bogue* in the central Atlantic in June 1943. The boat is being hit by a depth charge and cannon fire.

annihilation was the shortage of U-boats. Many had to be kept in home waters for training, others needed maintenance, while anti-submarine measures and accidents were taking a steady toll.

The hard-pressed Allied navies had time to improve the convoy organisation and to build and convert more escort vessels. In addition deep minefields were laid in the English Channel to force U-boats to make the lengthy northern passage to their hunting grounds. The Dover Barrage had taken most of World War I to perfect, but this time it worked completely, accounting for three out of four U-boats in the first month.

NORWEGIAN CAMPAIGN

British and French submarines were active in the North Sea, but the lack of major targets meant that they were limited to reconnaissance, minelaying and the occasional rare shot at a U-boat on passage. The principal bases were at Blyth and Dundee on the east coast, where they were joined by the Polish *Wilk* and *Orzel* after their heroic dash to freedom from the Baltic. The Royal Navy's Mediterranean boats were brought home to form the new 3rd Flotilla at Harwich.

Their chance came in the Norwegian Campaign in April 1940, when an Anglo-French decision to interrupt the iron trade from Narvik to the Baltic coincided

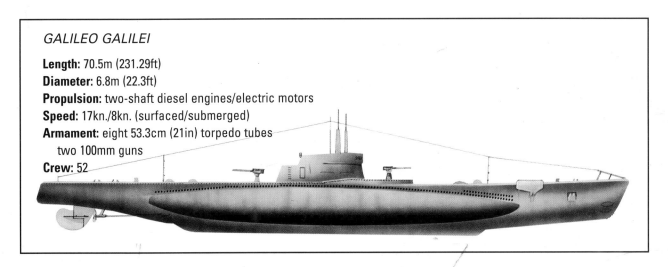

GALILEO GALILEI

Length: 70.5m (231.29ft)
Diameter: 6.8m (22.3ft)
Propulsion: two-shaft diesel engines/electric motors
Speed: 17kn./8kn. (surfaced/submerged)
Armament: eight 53.3cm (21in) torpedo tubes
   two 100mm guns
Crew: 52

Above: The *Galileo Galilei* was captured by a British trawler in the Red Sea and became HMS *X2*. Her sister, *Galileo Ferraris*, was sunk off Gibraltar.

with a German invasion of Denmark and Norway. The Admiralty had 19 submarines on patrol in the area, but the sinking of the troop transport *Rio de Janeiro* by the *Orzel* did nothing to rouse the Admiralty from its complacency. Allied submarines were given permission to attack only military transports on 9 April, but two days later the rules were changed to allow any ship to be attacked up to 10 miles from the coast of Norway. The spectacular results which followed showed what might have been achieved if the submarines had been alerted earlier. In less than a month 18 German transports, tankers and other mercantile vessels were sunk, as well as the light cruiser *Karlsruhe*, the gunnery training ship *Brummer* while *U.1*. Submarine-laid mines accounted for

another 13 ships, and the 'pocket-battleship' *Lützow* was badly damaged by HMS *Spearfish*. The British losses were not unduly heavy, bearing in mind that 101,605 tonnes (100,000 tons) of scarce German shipping was sunk: HMS *Thistle* was torpedoed by *U.4*, the *Tarpon* and *Sterlet* were sunk by anti-submarine vessels, and the minelayer *Seal* was forced to the surface and surrendered after suffering damage from one of her own mines.

To strengthen the minelaying effort the Admiralty asked the French Navy to lend three 'Saphir' class minelayers, but only the *Rubis* was made available. She arrived at Harwich on 1 May 1940, under the command of Lieutenant de Vaisseau Georges Cabanier, and laid 32 mines off Egersund nine days

Below: The Type XXI 'Electric Boat' was one of the weapons Admiral Dönitz hoped would counter U-boat losses suffered in 1943, but too few were built.

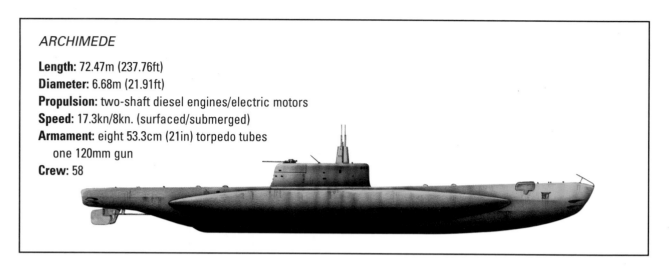

ARCHIMEDE

Length: 72.47m (237.76ft)
Diameter: 6.68m (21.91ft)
Propulsion: two-shaft diesel engines/electric motors
Speed: 17.3kn/8kn. (surfaced/submerged)
Armament: eight 53.3cm (21in) torpedo tubes
    one 120mm gun
Crew: 58

later, followed by 32 more on 24 May near Haugesund. Another dozen French submarines were in British waters, but none could match the achievements of the *Rubis*, and the *Doris* fell victim to *U.9* off the Dutch coast in May.

The comparatively poor performance of the U-boats can be explained by the failure of the magnetic pistol of the G7a torpedo. It was adversely affected by fluctuations in the earth's magnetism in high latitudes, but pre-war trials had not revealed the weakness. After bitter complaints from U-boat commanders Admiral Dönitz was forced to order a searching enquiry into the design and manufacture of the *Kriegsmarine*'s torpedoes. As the U-boats were withdrawn from the Atlantic for the Norwegian Campaign, the Allied escorts won a useful respite at a critical time.

The lull was illusory. While the Germans were consolidating their gains in Norway the main forma-

Below: Originally numbered *V4*, this large boat was the only specialised submarines minelayer built for the US Navy. The design was influenced by early U-boats.

Above: The Italian *Archimede* replaced an earlier submarine of the same name secretly transferred to the Nationalists during the Spanish Civil War

tions of the *Wehrmacht* and the *Luftwaffe* were preparing to invade France and the Low Countries. As soon as the Germans attacked through Belgium most of the Allied submarines were withdrawn from Norwegian waters and redeployed to prevent a naval incursion into the southern North Sea. The fall of Holland and the collapse of French resistance meant that a number of Dutch and French submarines fled to British ports. Strenuous efforts were made to get incomplete submarines out of Brest and Cherbourg, and the final total included the giant *Surcouf*, the small *Junon*, *Minerve*, *Narval*, *Ondine* and *Orion* and the incomplete *la Créole*. Under the armistice signed by Marshal Petain, French naval officers were ordered to take their ships back to France, but the British had good reason to doubt the validity of Hitler's guarantees. On 3 July, British naval personnel took over all French warships lying in British ports, the results varying according to

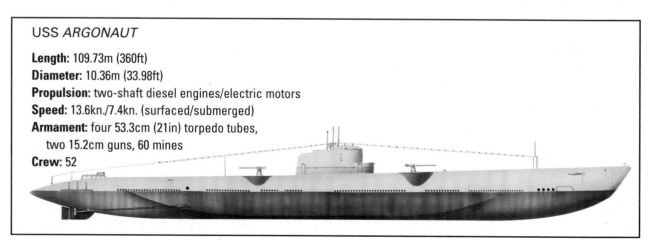

USS *ARGONAUT*

Length: 109.73m (360ft)
Diameter: 10.36m (33.98ft)
Propulsion: two-shaft diesel engines/electric motors
Speed: 13.6kn./7.4kn. (surfaced/submerged)
Armament: four 53.3cm (21in) torpedo tubes,
    two 15.2cm guns, 60 mines
Crew: 52

the tact and personalities involved. At Dundee, Commander Gambier RN won over the commander and crew of the *Rubis*, and a similar handover occurred at Portsmouth, but at Plymouth resistance to the commandeering of the *Surcouf* led to bloodshed. The formation of the Free French Navy under General de

Below: The giant Japanese submarines *I-400*, *I-401* and *I-14* alongside a US Navy tender in Tokyo Bay after the Japanese surrender in August 1945. The catapult tracks and cylindrical hangars for floatplanes can be seen. These large submarines found no use, and after the war were scuttled by the Americans.

Above: The Japanese *No.69* was a second-class submarine based on a Vickers design and the Royal Navy 'L' class. From 1940 she was used for training purposes.

Gaulle's government-in-exile allowed French naval personnel to fight on in French uniforms.

Within hours of the fall of France, Admiral Dönitz and his staff were ready with plans to exploit the dramatic developments. Road transport was commandeered to move heavy equipment such as air-compressors and torpedoes from Germany down to the French Atlantic coast. From here the U-boats could reach the crowded shipping lanes far more easily than before.

THE BATTLE OF THE ATLANTIC

The U-boats had completely outflanked their opponents, and in addition the British no longer had the help of most of the French Navy and the large mercantile marine. What Winston Churchill was to call the Battle of the Atlantic can be said to have started in earnest at this point. It was to be waged with no quarter given, right to the end of the war in Europe in 1945.

Ever the opportunist, Mussolini declared war on Britain and France, and to support his Axis partner he ordered the Italian Navy to set up a submarine base at Bordeaux. Under the name BETASOM (Beta [Bordeaux] Som [Sommergibili]) the new command had 27 submarines by the beginning of 1941. Had the Italian boats been better suited to Atlantic conditions

their contribution might have been decisive, but they achieved much less than the U-boats. Operating mainly off the Azores, they sank 1,016,050 tonnes (about 1 million tons) of shipping between January 1941 and September 1943, an average of 31,497 tonnes (31,000 tons) for each of the 33 boats involved. By comparison the 14 Type IXB boats there sank 40 per cent more.

After the relocation of the U-boats to France, Dönitz was able to form eight flotillas, all under Operation Area West:

1st U-boat Flotilla –	Brest (formerly at Kiel)
2nd U-boat Flotilla –	la Rochelle (from Wilhelmshaven)
3rd U-boat Flotilla –	la Pallice (from Kiel)
6th U-boat Flotilla –	St Nazaire (from Danzig)
7th U-boat Flotilla –	Brest/St Nazaire (from Kiel)
9th U-boat Flotilla –	Brest (newly formed)
10th U-boat Flotilla –	Lorient (newly formed)
12th U-boat Flotilla –	Bordeaux (newly formed)

The 4th and 5th Flotillas remained in Germany, while the 11th and 13th were based in Norway. As already mentioned, the Type VII proved to be on the small side for operating so far out into the Atlantic, and special 'milch-cow' U-boat tankers were designed. These Type XIV boats could transfer 438.9 tonnes (432 tons) of diesel fuel and four spare torpedoes to other U-boats in mid-ocean. Only 10 were completed

in 1941–2, and as they attracted the special attention of Allied anti-submarine patrols they were all early casualties. The bigger Type IX boats had sufficient endurance, but were slow to dive, making them vulnerable in the Western Approaches. They were therefore employed well away from the main trade routes, where many of their victims were unescorted. Largely because of these special conditions the Type IXB boats accounted for some 10 per cent of the entire mercantile tonnage sunk by U-boats.

Between June and November 1940 British and neutral shipping losses from submarine attack rose to 1,625,680 tonnes (1.6 million tons). It was the heyday of a new generation of 'ace' commanders, men like Prien and Kretschmer, who sank more than 203,210 tonnes (200,000 tons) apiece. K/Lt Otto Kretschmer in U.99 was the leading exponent of a brilliant tactic – the night attack on the surface. Taking advantage of her low silhouette and relatively high speed on diesel motors, a U-boat could penetrate the columns of the convoy itself, able to fire torpedoes and escape undetected. It required great courage to play hide-and-seek with large merchant ships, but the tactic usually threw the convoy into confusion. Only the growing use of radar put an end to this trick, but in 1940 hardly any escorts had radar.

DÖNITZ'S WOLF-PACKS

Even the depredations of the 'aces' were insufficient for Dönitz, who realised there would never be time to train a new generation of U-boat captains of the calibre of Kretschmer, Frauenheim, Schepke and the rest. Instead he implemented an idea first tried in 1918 by Commodore Bauer – the mass-attack or *Rüdeltaktik* (Wolf-pack tactics). In theory a force of 20 or more U-boats could swamp a convoy's defences. Dönitz envisaged seven steps in the process:

- A 'pack' of U-boats is disposed in a wide curve across the probable path of a convoy
- Any U-boat sighting the convoy signals its course, speed and composition, as well as its own position, to U-boat HQ
- The U-boat then shadows the convoy without attacking, merely reporting changes in course and speed
- U-boat HQ orders the rest of the pack to make contact with U-boat No.1
- When the pack is in place a coordinated attack is made on the convoy after dark
- At daybreak the pack breaks off its attack, leaving one shadower to maintain contact, allowing the

Above: The bow of the USS *Archerfish* surfaces from the depths. The 40mm Bofors gun in the foreground is typical of the anti-aircraft armament of US submarines in the war.

rest to recharge batteries and reload torpedo tubes
- At nightfall the pack attacks once more.

The appeal of wolf-pack tactics was simplicity. They made the best use of newly trained and relatively inexperienced commanders and crews. Inevitably these attacks wrought havoc among the poorly escorted convoys when the new system was phased in between October 1940 and March 1941.

ALLIED TACTICS

In fact the wolf-packs were unavoidable because the British and Canadian escorts were beginning to eliminate many of the 'aces'. In March 1941, the escorts got Prien in *U.47*, and then Schepke in *U.100* and Kretschmer in *U.99*, all sunk while attacking convoys. It was a heavy blow for the U-boat Arm, for these three commanders had sunk 111 ships between them, a total of 508,025 tonnes (over 500,000 tons). They and others fell victim to new weapons and tactics, notably new lightweight radars, high-frequency direction-finding ('Huff-Duff'), improved depth-charges, the first acoustic homing torpedoes, and finally, better coordination with shore-based patrol aircraft.

There was another way to exploit an inherent weakness of the U-boats' command system: eaves-

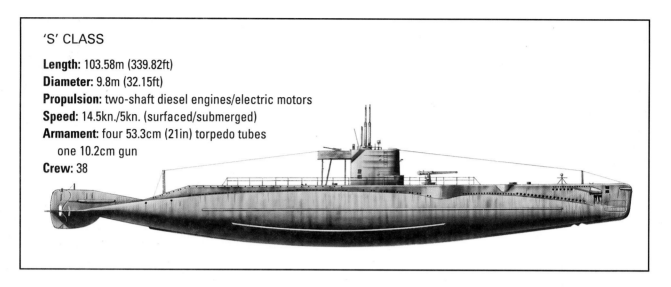

'S' CLASS

Length: 103.58m (339.82ft)
Diameter: 9.8m (32.15ft)
Propulsion: two-shaft diesel engines/electric motors
Speed: 14.5kn./5kn. (surfaced/submerged)
Armament: four 53.3cm (21in) torpedo tubes
   one 10.2cm gun
Crew: 38

dropping on the dense message-traffic between U-boat HQ and the individual U-boats at sea. British cryptographers at Bletchley Park had been working assiduously on the German Enigma machine-ciphers, and under the code-name 'Ultra' the information was disseminated to key sectors of the armed forces, in this case the U-boat Tracking Room at the Admiralty in London. The first major break into the naval ciphers occurred in May 1941, allowing the Tracking Room to identify individual U-boat call signs and to alert the escorts. Although there were periodic 'blackouts', when the codebreakers were defeated by a change in the cipher, the quality of 'Ultra' information became steadily better as the Battle of the Atlantic progressed. At sea, where ciphers could not be broken, the use of 'Huff-Duff' enabled escorts to pinpoint the source of radio transmissions to within a quarter of a mile.

The surest means of dealing with shadowers was to maintain an aircraft patrol astern of the convoy; if the U-boat was forced to dive it could not keep up and could no longer transmit reports. Until the end of 1941 there were neither aircraft nor carriers to spare for the 'Black Gap' in mid-Atlantic, but in mid-1941 the Admiralty started the conversion of an 'escort carrier' – a small merchant ship with a wooden flight deck. When the United States came into the war in December 1941 the country's enormous resources enabled many of these 'jeep carriers' to be built.

THE SNORKEL

To reduce the unbearable losses inflicted by radar-equipped escorts and aircraft, U-boat designers resuscitated an idea they had found in captured Dutch submarines in 1940. The *schnorchel* (nostril) was an air mast, originally intended to ventilate the interior of

Above: The numerous 'S' class was the US Navy's last series of submarine designs produced in World War I, but they were no better than their foreign contemporaries.

the boat, but in 1943 it promised a way to allow a U-boat to recharge its batteries without surfacing. The diesel-generators could be run at full power, while a masthead float valve prevented water from flooding the boat (small amounts of water were vented outboard). Used in rough weather it caused extreme discomfort to the crew by causing rapid changes in air pressure, but the alternative was destruction.

In practice the *schnorchel* (later Americanised to 'snorkel') did some damage to morale, and some of the inexperienced U-boat commanders were reluctant to use it for long periods. Radar warning receivers were used to detect hostile transmissions, but the performance of Allied radars outpaced the German scientists' efforts to counter them. Rubber coatings were used to absorb sonar energy and the *pillenwerfer* bubble decoy was introduced. It functioned like a giant Alka Seltzer, producing flat bubbles in the water, but experienced asdic operators rarely mistook them for genuine targets.

AXIS SUCCESSES

In the Mediterranean the Italian submarines scored some successes, torpedoing the cruisers HMS *Bonaventure*, HMS *Calypso* and HMS *Coventry* in 1940–1, but it was in the realm of special operations that they performed most spectacularly. The *maiale* (pigs) were known as 'human torpedoes', but they are more correctly described as swimmer delivery-vehicles. Carried to the scene of operations in cylinders welded to the decks of conventional submarines, they

penetrated the defences of Alexandria in December 1941 and the swimmers put heavy charges under the battleships HMS *Queen Elizabeth* and HMS *Valiant*. Unfortunately the Italians' bravery did not achieve the effect it deserved; the British ships settled on the mud of the harbour, and aerial reconnaissance reported that they were not immobilised. An even more audacious operation was mounted by *maiale* from an old tanker in the neutral Spanish port of Algeciras. Using a specially converted secret underwater compartment, the two-man crews mounted several attacks on British shipping in the harbour at Gibraltar.

British submarines were very active, from their exposed base at Malta and from Beirut and Alexandria. When the German and Italian air attacks made Malta's Grand Harbour virtually untenable, submarines ran essential cargoes of spares and ammunition. During the day they rested on the bottom of the harbour to reduce the risk from bombs. Once the siege of Malta was lifted in August 1942 the submarine flotilla was brought back to full strength to play its part in inter-rupting convoys between Italy and North Africa.

In 1941 Hitler ordered Dönitz to release 12 U-boats to the Mediterranean to take the pressure off the Italians. Although Dönitz gloomily predicted (correctly) that his precious U-boats would never return, they made their mark quickly, torpedoing the famous carrier HMS *Ark*

Royal and the old battleship HMS *Barham* in November 1941, followed by the carrier HMS *Eagle* in 1942.

When the United States entered the war most people thought that the U-boats would soon suffer greater losses. Sadly the US Navy refused to accept British recommendations about convoys, and the U-boats enjoyed six months of 'Happy Time' on the East Coast. Shore lights blazed and unescorted ships were sunk with impunity, while the same 'hunting groups' which had proved useless in 1916–17 dashed aimlessly from one sinking to another.

But the US shipyards were able to build merchant ships faster than the U-boats could sink them, and at the same time build hundreds of escorts. By the end of 1942 it seemed that the U-boats might be held, but during that year they sank 66,043,250 tonnes (65 million tons), and 212 U-boats were at sea by December.

The climax of the Battle of the Atlantic might have happened in the autumn of 1942, but escort carriers and support groups were withdrawn to cover the invasion of North Africa in November. Dönitz immediately sensed the slackening of the Allied effort in the Atlantic, but his U-boats were rendered less effective

Below: USS *Harder* off Mare Island Navy Yard, California, February 1944. Unlike many of her sisters of the 'Gato' class, her deck armament is comparatively austere.

by the severe winter conditions. As soon as the weather improved in March 1943 the U-boats struck with renewed ferocity. In the first big battle two groups of U-boats tried to trap convoy SC-121. Thirteen ships were sunk in five days, but the remainder slipped through a gap in the patrol line. Later that month Dönitz succeeded in concentrating 40 U-boats against convoys SC-122 and HX-229. In the first eight hours 12 ships were torpedoed, *U.338* managing to sink four with only five torpedoes. In a desperate attempt to stop the slaughter the senior escort commander ordered the two convoys to combine, and the survivors escaped. Some 142,247 tonnes (140,000 tons) had been lost, in return for only one U-boat. In the first 20 days of March 508,025 tonnes (500,000 tons) was sunk, and the Admiralty was seriously considering abandoning the trusted convoy system. Dönitz seemed about to make good his boast that the U-boat alone would win the war.

Help was on its way, however, as the escort forces released from the North African invasion were thrown

Above: An officer at the periscope of his submarine during training at the New London Submarine Base, Connecticut, in preparation for the war in the Pacific against Japan.

back into the Atlantic battle. Allied scientists were also winning the technology battle, and Bletchley Park mastered the latest U-boat cipher in the nick of time. In March 1943, 15 U-boats were sunk, followed by 16 in April, but in May a staggering 41 were sunk. Defeat was conceded later that month, when Dönitz announced the need to 'regroup' and re-equip. The U-boats remained dangerous to the end, but they never regained the upper hand. Although new designs took shape in 1944 the Third Reich was crumbling, and production problems ensured that only three of the vaunted Type XXI 'electro U-boats' were operational when Germany surrender unconditionally.

Dr Walter had even more advanced ideas, the use of a thermal fuel, high-test peroxide (HTP, known to the Germans as Perhydrol), to generate its own oxygen for

air-independent propulsion. The system was unreliable, not least because Perhydrol was a lethally unsafe fuel, liable to burn spontaneously and capable of corroding cloth, flesh and even metal. Despite these drawbacks the Type XVIIB was put into production, and a few prototypes were ready by the end of the war.

US SUBMARINES IN THE PACIFIC

When the Japanese Navy attacked Pearl Harbor in December 1941 the Pacific Fleet submarines were suddenly in the front line. Apart from the three carriers which had escaped the disaster, there was little that Admiral Chester W Nimitz could do to take the offensive against the Imperial Japanese Navy. The old 'S' class boats in the Philippines were not suited to Pacific conditions, but the latest 'Gato' class were formidable long-range boats with a heavy armament of six bow tubes and four stern tubes, and a 12.7cm (5in) deck gun. The design proved well suited to the Pacific, and only minor improvements were made in the light of war experience. Their successors, the 'Balao' and 'Tench' classes, were virtually repeats, but capable of diving deeper because of their stronger hulls.

US submarines in the Pacific carried out a range of missions. Their prime targets were aircraft carriers, followed by tankers, and then other warships and mercantile vessels, but they also reported on Japanese ship movements, laid mines, rescued downed aircrew and reconnoitred invasion beaches. Unfortunately they suffered initially from a major drawback – like the German U-boats in 1940 the magnetic pistols of their torpedoes were faulty. Getting the designers to admit that anything was wrong took a long time, and it had the deleterious effect of weakening the confidence of the submariners in their equipment. On the plus side, Japanese anti-submarine warfare proved to be less effective than predicted, not least because the Imperial Japanese Navy believed that commerce protection was less 'honourable' than engaging warships. This is not to say that the Japanese submarines did not achieve any successes, but that they never matched the expectations of the pre-war planners. Their greatest successes were achieved in the fighting around the Solomon Islands. The carrier USS *Saratoga* was badly damaged on 31 August 1942, and the USS *Wasp* was sunk three weeks later. The battleship USS *North Carolina* was hit on the same day, 15 September, reducing the heavy units to a single carrier and a battleship.

The US Navy had no such romantic illusions. After Pearl Harbor, Japan's mercantile marine had grown by 812,840 tonnes (800,000 tons) by the addition of captured ships, until it totalled 6,096,300 tonnes (6 million tons). It was barely sufficient to meet the needs of the new sprawling maritime empire, but the Navy regarded this as a bottomless purse from which to draw tonnage for naval auxiliaries. Little or nothing was done to replace the 1,016,050 tonnes (1 million tons) lost in 1942, and it was not until August 1943, when losses had risen to 2,032,100 tonnes (2 million tons), that alarm bells began to ring in Tokyo. US submarine commanders had priorities: carriers, tankers and merchant ships, in that order.

As radar was progressively fitted to Pacific Fleet submarines their effectiveness increased noticeably. A submarine could stalk its prey on the surface, fire a torpedo and then move away rapidly before the escorts had time to react. Some daring submariners perfected the 'down the throat shot', a highly risky way of attacking escorts. The submarine commander allowed the escort to start its depth-charging run against its target, and then destroyed it with a full bow salvo of six torpedoes at short range.

If the German U-boats had ever been able to treat Allied escorts with such disdain in the Atlantic or the Mediterranean, the outcome of World War II would have been very different. The US submarines adopted their own variant of the 'wolf-pack', hunting groups of three boats, identified by their senior officers: 'Ben's Busters', 'Donk's Devils', 'Ed's Eradicators', 'Laughlin's Loopers', and so on. Several boats like the USS *Barb*, USS *Rasher* and USS *Silversides* exceeded 914,445 tonnes (90,000 tons) each, while the top-scoring USS *Tang* sank 101,839 tonnes (100,231 tons). The price was heavy, 59 sunk by all causes, including grounding. But the Japanese told American interrogators after the war that they had accounted for 486 US Navy submarines! This discrepancy points to something much more serious than a misjudgement on countermeasures.

JAPAN'S FRAGILE EMPIRE

Japan imported 20 per cent of its food, 24 per cent of its coal, 88 per cent of its iron ore and 90 per cent of its oil, making its fragile maritime empire exceedingly vulnerable to attack. By the end of 1943 the total shipping lost was 3,048,150 tonnes (nearly 3 million tons), most of it sunk by submarines. The depredations continued in 1944, with nearly 1,016,050 tonnes (1,000,000 tons) sunk in the first five months. As the Japanese were forced to rely more and more on small junks and coasters for moving cargoes, the big

American submarines found themselves short of targets. To deny coastal waters to the Japanese the Royal Navy and the Royal Netherlands Navy established three flotillas in the Far East. The smaller British and Dutch submarines were able to operate inside the 28m (91.86ft) line, and they soon began to make themselves felt. In addition to many minor mercantile craft, these boats sank the cruisers *Ashigara* and *Kuma*.

The American submarines' greatest military successes were the sinking of the new carrier *Taiho* by the USS *Albacore* during the Battle of the Philippine Sea in June 1944 and the giant ex-battleship carrier conversion, the *Shinano*, by the USS *Archerfish* in the Inland Sea in November 1944. Their crucial reconnaissance role was shown to best effect on the eve of the Battle of Leyte Gulf in October 1944. The USS *Darter* and USS *Drum* ambushed a heavy cruiser squadron, sinking the *Atago* and *Maya* and damaging the *Takao*.

As the war progressed the huge Japanese submarine fleet seemed to lose direction. On 19 May 1944, acting on intercepted Japanese orders, the destroyer escort USS *England* encountered a patrol line off the Solomons. She sank *I.16* northeast of Choiseul Island. Three days later she sank *RO.106* off Kavieng in New Ireland, followed by *RO.104* on 23 May, *RO.116* on 24 May, *RO.108* on 26 May and finally *RO.105* on 31 May. The Imperial Navy turned to desperate measures, sacrificing submarines in useless attacks on invasion fleets and running supplies and ammunition to outlying garrisons. A special supply-submarine design was developed, the 'I.361' class, capable of carrying

Above: USS *Argonaut*, second of the name, in April 1945. The forward deck gun has given way to a short 5in gun abaft the conning tower, a 40mm Bofors and twin 20mm guns aft.

83.3 tonnes (82 tons) of cargo and having a surfaced endurance of 27,780km (15,000 miles). The Army even built its own supply-submarines, and a number of Navy boats were converted to carry 'Kaiten' midget submarines. The most ambitious project was the giant 'I.400' class, ordered in 1942. They were the biggest submarines built up to that time, 189m (620ft) long and equipped with four small floatplane bombers (three plus the component parts of a fourth). The 'I.14' design was slightly smaller, and could operate two floatplanes. The original role for these extraordinary craft was a bombing raid on the Panama Canal.

The end of the war against Japan in August 1945 also marked the end of the most successful submarine campaign in history. Only 231 Japanese merchant ships survived out of a pre-war total of 2337 listed in Lloyds' Register. In all, 190 Japanese submarines were delivered by August 1945, but only 55 were surrendered, a loss-rate of more than 70 per cent and a heavy price to pay for so little.

MIDGET SUBMARINES

Although the Italians had pioneered the midget submarine in World War I, the most work between the wars was done by the Japanese, who intended to use them to attack defended harbours. Yet the attempt to penetrate Pearl Harbor in conjunction with the carrier

air strikes was a dismal failure, with four sunk. An attempt to attack Sydney Harbour in May 1942 was also unsuccessful, although a torpedo intended for the heavy cruiser USS *Chicago* sank a ferry. An almost simultaneous attack on a British invasion force at Diego Suarez in Madagascar had more success, with two midgets damaging the battleship HMS *Ramillies* and an oiler. It was also one of the few occasions when a submarine-launched floatplane achieved its aim; *I.10*'s floatplane had reconnoitred the anchorage a day earlier.

In 1944, a growing realisation that the Empire of the Rising Sun was staring defeat in the face led to the production of large numbers of 'Kairyu' and 'Kaiten' types. The 'Kaiten' was a Type 93, 60cm (23.6in) 'Long Lance' torpedo body adapted for human guidance, whereas the 'Kairyu' carried conventional torpedoes slung underneath the hull. Although hundreds were built, they achieved few successes.

The Italians also revived the idea of midgets, but they are best remembered for the *maiale* mentioned

Below: The 'Gato' class USS *Peto* running at speed. The limber holes in the outer casing are to assist rapid flooding and venting and to release water trapped in the casing.

earlier. These made such an impression on the Royal Navy that an equivalent, the 'Chariot', was produced. Ironically, their greatest successes were in the hands of Italian operators when used to attack former Italian warships under German control. The British also built X-craft and Welman craft. Instead of torpedoes the four-man X-craft and its Far East equivalent, the air-conditioned XE-craft, carried a pair of 2.03-tonne (2-ton) charges faired into the saddle tanks. They were used with great effect against the battleship *Tirpitz* in a Norwegian fjord in September 1943, inflicting permanent damage. Two XE-craft put the heavy cruiser *Takao* out of action in Singapore in July 1945.

Like their Japanese allies the Germans produced large numbers of *Kleine kampfmittel* (small assault units) in a vain attempt to fend off invasion. Known as *Neger* (negro), *Marder* (marten), *Biber* (beaver), *Molch* (salamander) and *Seehund* (seadog), they were first deployed at the Anzio landings in 1944 and scored a few successes off the Normandy beaches. They were also used to attack Allied shipping in the Schelde estuary in late 1944. The *Seehund* was the most successful, and sank a Free French escort destroyer and a British tank landing ship in the Thames Estuary as late as February 1945.

Cold War Beneath the Waves

Under Stalin the Soviet Navy built up a powerful fleet of conventional and nuclear submarines, creating the risk of Europe being cut off from American reinforcements. On both sides submarines developed fast, culminating in the awesome power of the nuclear submarine armed with long-range nuclear-tipped missiles.

When the Third Reich collapsed in May 1945, teams of American, British and Russian submarine experts converged on German dockyards to locate and recover every scrap of information about the latest U-boat designs. In particular they wanted details of the Type XXI and the even more advanced HTP-driven Type XVII. The Americans and British raised two Type XVIIBs and put them back into service for trials, while the Russians took several hull sections away.

Left: The 'Los Angeles' class nuclear attack submarine USS *City of Corpus Christi* at moderate speed. Modern submarine hulls are optimised for submerged performance.

It was 1918 all over again, with the victors almost coming to blows over their shares of the loot. In the end the Americans and British got the lion's share because their armies had overrun the principal shipyards and factories in the West. In all, nearly 40 U-boats were incorporated into various navies, some for trials but others as part of the postwar fleet.

Although the Walter turbine was of great interest, it proved unreliable and offered only limited endurance at great cost. Only the Royal Navy went to the lengths of building HTP boats postwar in an effort to make the system work, and for a while its two experimental boats, HMS *Excalibur* and HMS *Explorer*, established

Above: The USS *Seawolf* was the second prototype SN in the US Navy, using the S2G sodium-cooled reactor. She was later re-engined with a pressurised water S2Wa plant.

a new underwater speed record by exceeding 27 knots. The Type XXI offered a more useful line of enquiry, although the influence of the design itself has been greatly exaggerated by a number of historians and analysts. But there were a number of problems: the hull form had not been tank-tested and proved unstable in service, the internal arrangement of equipment was far from ideal, and there were serious weaknesses in construction. Although the Soviet Navy built a number of boats which closely resembled the Type XXI, the Royal Navy and the US Navy were happier to adapt the best features to fit in with their own designs. Thus the concepts of the Type XXI – the large-capacity batteries and the mechanical reloading gear for the torpedo tubes – became standard around the world.

THE GUPPY PROGRAMME

In 1946, the US Navy began its Greater Underwater Propulsive Power (GUPPY) programme, upgrading the large number of 'Gato', 'Balao' and 'Tench' class boats built during the war.

The basic elements of the GUPPY conversion included streamlining the hull and augmenting underwater power. The prototypes *Odax* and *Pomodon* were originally intended to act as fast targets for training surface anti-submarine forces, and to cope with an expected improvement of performance in Soviet submarines. The conning tower was replaced by a streamlined 'sail', which enclosed periscopes and snorkel mast. The characteristic buoyant bow (intended to improve surface performance) was replaced by a round bow, and every possible piece of equipment likely to cause resistance was either removed or made retractable. It was not easy to find space internally for more battery cells because the wartime fleet boats were by no means spacious. The solution was to remove the auxiliary diesel-generator from the after-engine room and reposition it in the space formerly occupied by the magazine for the redundant deck-gun.

Much work had to be done on battery technology to achieve higher output. By accepting a shorter life (18 months) and designing a smaller battery-cell, it was possible to provide four main batteries of 126 cells each (the original boats had only two). This brought new problems, for the high-capacity batteries generated more hydrogen and heat, increasing the risk of fire and explosion. After experimenting with a closed-cell system the US Navy reverted to a water-cooled open-cell system, and the air-conditioning equipment was boosted by nearly 300 percent to handle the extra load.

Apart from minor teething troubles the GUPPY I conversion proved successful. A simultaneous

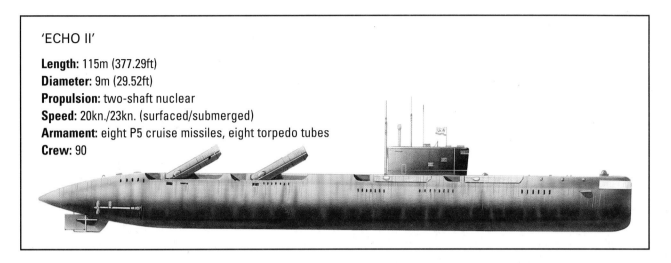

'ECHO II'

Length: 115m (377.29ft)
Diameter: 9m (29.52ft)
Propulsion: two-shaft nuclear
Speed: 20kn./23kn. (surfaced/submerged)
Armament: eight P5 cruise missiles, eight torpedo tubes
Crew: 90

programme to improve the snorkel was running at Portsmouth Navy Yard in New Hampshire. The basic problem was that exhausting gases underwater created more back-pressure than the diesels could handle. The American two-cycle diesels suffered pressure fluctuations when the float valve closed, whereas the wartime German four-cycle diesels were not badly affected. Some components of the Fairbanks Morse and General Motors diesels were redesigned to cope with the stresses, but the ultimate solution was to replace the simple float valve with an air-actuated head valve designed to act rapidly and positively. The opening and closing was now controlled by three electrodes located near the snorkel head. When a wave broke over the head it completed a circuit, directing air to shut the valve.

The exhaust mast was designed to be raised with the induction mast, and to ride about 1.21–2.4m (4–8ft) below the surface. The exhaust port was fitted with baffles to reduce the amount of smoke and haze

Above: The 29 Project 675 SSGNs were built in the 1960s to provide a means of attacking cities in the United States. The P-5 missile could not be used against ships.

reaching the surface. A mast similar to that in the Type XXI boats was tried in the USS *Irex* in 1947, but it threw up a highly visible plume of spray. The US Navy boats, being much larger than the U-boats, needed a much bigger snorkel head and mast to draw in sufficient air, and a major redesign of the head was needed to reduce the plume. Three types of snorkel were developed: the original GUPPY I type; a simpler type for the unmodernised fleet boats, and a sophisticated type for fast attack boats. Even nuclear submarines need snorkels; they are needed if the boat is running on the auxiliary diesel-electric system, and

Below: The Project 667A 'Yankee' type SSBNs followed US Navy practice for the first time, siting the SS-N-6 'Sawfly' missiles in vertical launch tubes abaft the sail.

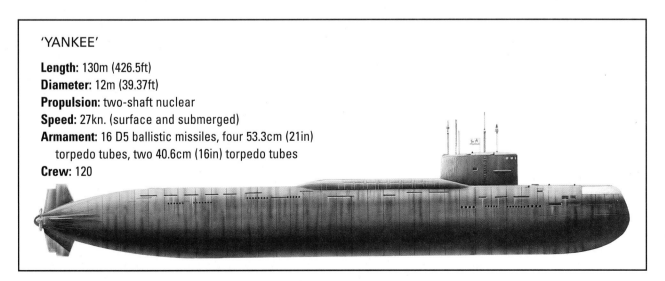

'YANKEE'

Length: 130m (426.5ft)
Diameter: 12m (39.37ft)
Propulsion: two-shaft nuclear
Speed: 27kn. (surface and submerged)
Armament: 16 D5 ballistic missiles, four 53.3cm (21in)
   torpedo tubes, two 40.6cm (16in) torpedo tubes
Crew: 120

Left: A Soviet Navy 'Echo II' class nuclear-armed submarine running trimmed down in the Ionian Sea. She was photographed after a collision with a US frigate.

The GUPPY concept was adopted by other navies. The Royal Navy converted its 'A' and 'T' classes along similar lines, lengthening the hulls to accommodate more batteries. The snorkel was also introduced, but nicknamed the 'snort', a copy of the German folding type. Only after the disastrous loss of HMS *Affray* in 1951, when her snort mast fractured, did the Royal Navy turn to the US Navy's telescopic type, which was enclosed by the sail.

In addition to the large GUPPY programme the US Navy experimented with novel uses for its fleet boats. In 1946 the *Requin* and *Spinax* went to sea with large radar antennae on deck and processing equipment below. As 'radar pickets' they were intended to detect hostile aircraft and direct defending fighters. These conversions and two more, the *Tigrone* and *Burrfish*, were never popular with their operators because of endless flooding of electrical circuits. Appropriately, the enquiry into their problems was codenamed Operation 'Migraine', but in spite of the severe

it is still the quickest way to rid the interior of the boat of the various contaminants which cannot be absorbed by the air-purification system.

The success of the *Odax* and *Pomodon* led to a further 22 'Balao' class boats being converted, but after further improvements all 24 were redesignated the GUPPY II type. In 1950, a cheaper and simpler GUPPY IA was authorised for ten more 'Balao' class, while the GUPPY IIA conversion (16 boats) included streamlining but substituted a bigger sonar installation for the two forward sets of machinery.

Below: USS *Skipjack* (SSN-585) was the first of a revolutionary class of SSNs using the advanced 'Albacore' hull to achieve maximum speed underwater.

Above: USS *Queenfish* was one of a new class of SSNs optimised for silent running and deep diving, exploiting the advantages of the 'Skipjack' class.

maintenance problems six more Gatos were converted, and three nuclear-powered equivalents were built before the idea was abandoned.

SUBMARINE-LAUNCHED MISSILES

Nothing had come of a German plan to tow submersible rafts across the Atlantic to bombard the United States with V-2 rockets, but the US Navy was determined to match the awesome power of long-range missiles to the submarine. In 1947, a submarine fired the first surface-to-surface cruise missile, the KUW-1 Loon (later renumbered LTV-N-2). This improved version of the German V-1 'doodlebug' was carried in a large water-tight cylindrical canister on deck, and launched from a collapsible ramp by a rocket booster. It was assembled on deck and then 'flown' by radio commands, either from the parent submarine or from another boat. The culmination of the programme was the conversion of two 'Gato' class, the *Carbonero* and *Cusk* in 1946, the first firing being made by the *Cusk* off Point Mugu on the Californian coast. Even more impressive was a test-firing in 1950, when the *Cusk* fired her Loon,

submerged and tracked the missile for 194.46km (105 miles), using AN/BPQ-2 guidance equipment.

It was the birth of the submarine-launched cruise missile. An improved Loon, the SSM-N-8A Regulus, made its maiden flight in 1950. The first Regulus-armed submarine, the USS *Tunny*, was commissioned in March 1953, and she and the *Barbero* could accommodate two missiles in a deck hangar. Regulus was a strategic weapon, and the five boats armed with the system were assigned to the Pacific Fleet to counter any threat from mainland China. An improved Regulus II was fired from the USS *Grayback* in 1958, but when the programme was cancelled that year she and her sister *Growler* and the nuclear boat *Halibut* were armed with Regulus I instead. The money saved was diverted to a much more powerful system, the Polaris submarine-launched ballistic missile (SLBM). Although supporters of the Regulus system scoffed at the risk of remaining on the surface to launch it, the submariners would be happier with a system launched from below the surface.

NUCLEAR REACTORS

All these experiments reflected the submarine community's search for ways to wring more life out of the wartime submarine fleet. Exotic applications included a submarine oiler, a cargo-carrier and amphibious

USS *NAUTILUS*

Length: 98.45m (323ft)
Diameter: 8.23m (27ft)
Propulsion: two-shaft nuclear steam turbines/electric motors
Speed: 18kn./20kn. (surfaced/submerged)
Armament: six 53.3cm (21in) torpedo tubes
Crew: 111

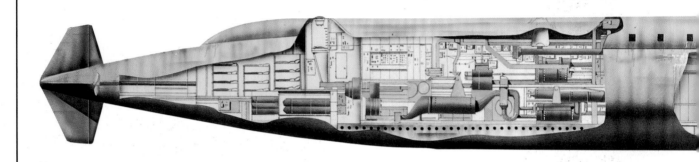

transports. But the Navy was already forging ahead with a scheme which would revolutionise undersea warfare. Work on a nuclear reactor plant for submarines started in 1948 – the Submarine Thermal Reactor (STR). This was developed by Westinghouse into the STR Mk 2 (later redesignated S2W) in collaboration with the Argonne National Laboratory. Development of the associated technology was in the hands of a group of scientists and engineers at the Naval Reactors Branch of the Atomic Energy Commission, led by a Captain Hyman G Rickover, USN. The penalty for failure would be immense; not only was a large amount of money at stake, but the prestige of the United States was involved. However, Rickover and his team never had any doubt.

On 12 December 1951, when the Department of the Navy was satisfied that the time had come to order a hull for the new nuclear plant, the name chosen was *Nautilus*. This commemorated not only two previous US submarines, but also Fulton's submersible and the mythical boat of Captain Nemo in the book *Twenty Thousand Leagues Under the Sea*. Her keel was laid on 14 June 1952, by President Truman at the Electric Boat Division of General Dynamics in Groton, Connecticut – the direct descendant of John P Holland's original company. Work progressed rapidly, the *Nautilus* (SSN-571) being launched on 21 January 1954 by Mrs Eisenhower and commissioned eight months later.

She was a great success, not least because the hull design was conventional to avoid unnecessary risk, and because Captain Rickover had stressed reactor safety as an absolute priority. In her first year the *Nautilus* steamed 114,824km (more than 62,000 miles). Apart from the streamlining of the hull, she was conventional in layout, with two shafts driven by steam turbines using superheated steam generated by the nuclear reactor via a heat-exchanger. By a strange quirk of history steam propulsion for submarines was finally vindicated.

Only recently has reliable information become public on the Soviet Navy's efforts to match the US Navy's achievement. Work on the first Soviet design began in September 1952, roughly four years behind the Americans. The team was headed by V M Peregudov and N A Dollezhal, with Academician A P Alexandrov as chief scientific adviser. Special Design Bureau 143 was assigned the task of turning the Project 627 design into reality in the spring of 1953. Detailed design work took only 18 months, and in the summer of 1958, *K.3* sailed on her sea trials. When the reactor plant 'went critical' on 4 July the Soviet Navy's nuclear fleet came into existence.

Known to NATO as the 'November' type , the new nuclear attack submarine (SSN) entered service as *K.3*, but was later named *Leninskii Komsomol* (Lenin's Young Communist League). She was followed by 12 more Project 627A boats, known to

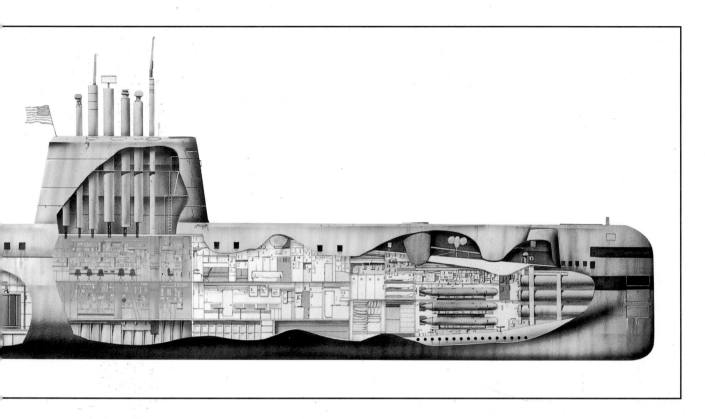

the Soviets as the 'Kit' class, and the same power plant was used in the Project 658 ('Hotel') and Project 659 ('Echo'), hence the Western nickname for the reactor plant, the HEN. Both 'Hotel' and 'Echo' were armed with long-range anti-ship missiles – SSGNs in US Navy standard nomenclature.

Above: *Nautilus* was the world's first nuclear-powered submarine. Its hull design was conservative though.

Below: The Project 661 design, known to Western intelligence as 'Papa', exceeded 44 knots on trials, but the plant was unreliable and the titanium hull too expensive.

Above: A close-up of the Soviet Project 671RTM 'Victor III' during the Cold War. The prominent 'pod' on the rudder is a dispenser for a towed array.

There was great alarm in the US Navy and NATO when the Soviet nuclear programme got under way so quickly, and even more when the performance of the 'Novembers' was monitored. But the Soviets were having trouble with the pressurised water reactor (PWR) HEN plant, and turned to liquid metal cooling. The Project 645 boat *K.27* was a 'November' with the prototype reactor cooled by lead-bismuth. It was successful, but had the serious operational drawback of making the SSN more dependent on shore support. For similar reasons the US Navy developed a liquid sodium-cooled plant for the *Seawolf* (SSN-575), but discovered that its disadvantages outweighed the benefits. Improvements in the design of PWRs provided the same results for less money.

RACE TO THE NORTH POLE

Of all the exploits of the *Nautilus*, none caught the imagination of the world better than her voyage to the North Pole. On 23 July 1958, she left Pearl Harbor,

heading for the Aleutian Islands and the Bering Sea. She surfaced briefly in the shallow Chukchi Sea and then dived to traverse the 3657m (12,000ft) deep Barrow Sea Valley. Two days later her commanding officer, Commander William R Anderson USN told his crew that they were at 90 degrees North, exactly over the Pole, but under a 16m (52.5ft) thick roof of ice. As a result, the world at large could not receive the news until 5 August, two days later, when she was able to transmit radio messages once more. Rising to the surface had been highly risky, and four previous attempts had been aborted. There was the obvious risk of collision by surfacing inadvertently under the icecap, or by hitting uncharted underwater obstacles. The *Nautilus* relied only on echo-sounders and an upward-looking TV camera.

Right: The Project 971 'Akula' class are the Russian Navy's current series-production SSNs. The design is noted for improved silencing and its torpedoes and cruise missiles.

The Soviet Union was determined not to be left behind in this underwater version of the space race. In July 1962, the *Leninskii Komsomol* (*K.3*) reached the North Pole, followed a year later by *K.181*. Also, in 1963, *K.133* circumnavigated the globe. But, in addition to these public displays of Soviet achievements, Special Design Bureau 143 had been working on a plan to arm the Project 627 design with the P-20 anti-ship cruise missile. Two projects, 627A and 653, were developed, but in 1960 work on both was stopped.

INTERMEDIATE-RANGE BALLISTIC MISSILE (IRBM)

As early as 1954 the Korolyov Bureau had been working on an intermediate-range ballistic missile (IRBM) capable of being launched from a submarine. On 16 September 1955 the diesel-electric submarine the converted 'Zulu' type *B.67* launched the R-11FM variant of the Army's 'Scud' (R-11) missile. Five more conversions followed, plus 23 newly built Project 629 ('Golf') class, armed with three improved R-13 (NATO SS-N-4) missiles.

The US Navy's early experiments with submarine-launched cruise missiles had taken it up a blind alley, but the prospect of mating the awesome destructive power of the IRBM with the nuclear submarine was irresistible. Throughout the 1950s the Pentagon remained obsessed with the possibility of a pre-emptive strike by Soviet bombers and missiles and its land-based intercontinental ballistic missile (ICBM) launch-sites. It was reasoned that a submarine-based deterrent would be immune to such a 'first strike', and could also act as a 'second strike' weapon after such an attack.

There were formidable technical problems to overcome, but certain factors made underwater launch feasible. For one thing, water is incompressible, and so a rocket can use the surface of the sea as a launching pad. A second advantage was that such a weapon need only be an IRBM, as no place on earth is more than 2735km (1700 miles) from the sea.

On the negative side, there was the difficulty of sustaining life in a submarine for months on end, and what was seen as the impossibility of fixing the submarine's position accurately enough to plot the coordinates for the firing of a ballistic (unguided) missile. These problems were common to all nuclear submarines, but they were critical for boats armed with ballistic missiles. To maintain an effective deterrent the submarine must remain out of touch for as

Below: The original Project 667B 'Delta I' SSBNs carried 12 SS-N-8 missiles, but 'Delta II' and 'Delta III' had four more missiles. 'Delta IV' had 16 R-29RM SS-N-23 missiles.

'DELTA I'

Length: 140m (459.31ft)
Diameter: 12m (39.37ft)
Propulsion: two-shaft nuclear
Speed: 25kn. (surfaced and submerged)
Armament: 12 D-9 ballistic missiles, six torpedo tubes
Crew: 120

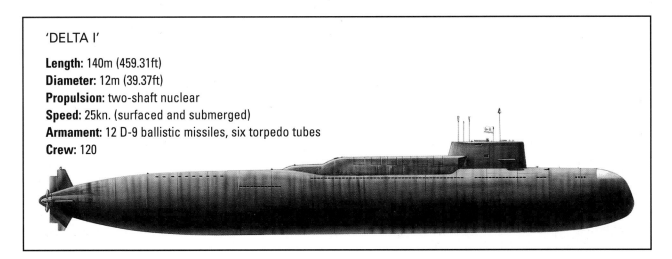

long as possible, only daring to put up an aerial to get a radio-transmitted navigational 'fix'.

Preliminary studies into ways of firing such missiles as the US Air Force's liquid-fuelled Jupiter had shown that the hazards of handling liquid fuel were unacceptable. Advances in solid fuel avoided that problem, and in 1956 the Secretary of the Navy authorised a start on a new SLBM project, codenamed Polaris.

POLARIS AND POSEIDON MISSILES

Scientists prophesied that idea would not work, and even some of the optimists thought that nothing would be achieved for 20 years. But President Kennedy sanctioned the additional funding needed to solve the technical problems, and on 20 July 1960 the USS *George Washington* (SSBN-598) fired two A1 Polaris rounds off Cape Canaveral, splashing down 2222km (1200 miles) away. The message from the submarine: "From out of the deep to target. Perfect", set the seal on

Below: HMS *Dreadnought*, the Royal Navy's first SSN, was driven by the same S5W reactor plant as the US Navy's 'Skipjack' class. She started sea trials in 1962.

the work of Hyman Rickover, now an admiral. Within a year, a second SSBN, the *Robert E Lee*, had established a new record, spending 68 days underwater.

Two important technical advances had made this possible. The Ship's Inertial Navigation System (SINS) provided for the first time a means to accurately compute a submarine's course without reference to Magnetic or True North. SINS plots all drift and movement in relation to a known datum point, and although it needs occasional updates to avoid 'drift', it provides sufficient accuracy for a nuclear-tipped missile. The habitability problem was solved by the development of 'scrubbers' to clean and filter the air, allowing the crew to breathe recycled air without ill-effects. The research also showed up the need for non-toxic paints in the submarine.

Polaris relied on six major elements:
- SINS, which enabled the fire control system to measure the distance between the submarine and its targets
- The computerised fire control system, which used information from SINS to compute a trajectory for each missile continuously

Above: HMS *Torbay* is a unit of the 'Trafalgar' class, currently the most modern SSNs in service with the Royal Navy. They are also being updated with new systems.

- Missile Test and Readiness Equipment (MTRE), which checked the readiness of each missile
- Launcher control, which prepared all 16 tubes for launch, equalising pressure to keep the tube free of water before the launch
- Memory in each missile's guidance system, which received and stored data from the fire control system
- Missile control panel, which reflected the status of all 16 missiles.

When the firing key was closed in the final sequence, a gas generator ignited to create the pressure needed to force the missile upwards from its tube. After leaving the tube the solid-fuel motor ignited, allowing the missile to enter its ballistic trajectory. In flight its inertial guidance system kept it on course without external commands.

In its day Polaris was the most deadly weapon ever taken to sea. The final A3 variant, with its three separate Multiple Independently-targeted Re-entry Vehicle (MIRV) nuclear warheads could deliver more explosive power than all the bombs dropped in World War II. A3 had a range of 5556km (nearly 3000 miles),

USS SKIPJACK

Length: 76.8m (251.96ft)
Diameter: 9.7m (31.82ft)
Propulsion: one-shaft nuclear
Speed: 30kn. (surfaced and submerged)
Armament: six 53.3cm (21in) torpedo tubes (bow)
Crew: 114

allowing the submarine a bigger area of sea in which to hide, and so complicating the problem for Soviet countermeasures. In fact both the US Navy and the Royal Navy (which bought A3 Polaris for four 'Resolution' class SSBNs) claim that none of their SSBNs was ever detected by Soviet submarines or anti-submarine forces.

In 1970, the USS *James Madison* (SSBN-627) launched the first C3 Poseidon. Although larger, it had the same range as A3 Polaris because its nose cone contained a number of 'penetration aids' such as decoys, to improve the chances of the warheads defeating the antiballistic missile (ABM) defences around Moscow. The grim arithmetic of nuclear deterrence had at its heart the conviction that only a guaranteed single hit from a ballistic missile resulting in the destruction of 62.5 per cent (five-eighths) of Moscow would deter the Soviet Union from attacking the West. Anything less might only goad the Politburo into continuing the exchange... We will never know if the calculation was correct.

OTHER NAVIES PRODUCE A RESPONSE

Although taken by surprise at the speed with which Polaris was tested and introduced into service, the Soviet Navy did not wait long to provide a response. In 1963, the first Project 651 (NATO's 'Juliett') appeared: the *K.156*. Sixteen of these diesel-electric submarines (SSGNs) were built, armed with four launch tubes for P-6 *Progress* (SS-N-3A 'Shaddock') missiles in the casing. These were raised to the firing position, a system repeated in the nuclear-powered Project 675 ('Echo') class. The 28 boats of this class had double the armament of the 'Juliett' design,

Above: The US Navy's 'Skipjack' class set new standards of performance, but the Westinghouse S5W nuclear plant was noisy and generally inhibited efficiency.

together with the benefit of nuclear propulsion, but the 555-km (300-mile) 'Shaddock' bore no comparison with Polaris.

The first SLBM in service was the R-13 (SS-N-4 'Sark') – developed for the Project 629 ('Golf') class and the Project 658 ('Hotel') class (three carried in the fin or sail). These boats were soon rearmed with the 650-mile R-21 'Serb' missile, but the Russian designers eventually produced an SSBN clearly influenced by the American boats. This was the Project 667A ('Yankee'), which appeared in 1967. They resembled the 'George Washington' class in layout, with 16 R-27 (SS-N-6 'Sawfly') missiles, credited with a range of 1500 miles.

The British and French followed American practice from the start, and the 'Resolution' and 'Redoubtable' classes were similarly configured. The Royal Navy bought the A3 Polaris, whereas the French *Marine Nationale* funded the French M2. The British were offered Polaris as a replacement for the cancelled Skybolt air-launched ballistic weapon, but General de Gaulle had quarrelled with the Americans, and the same deal was not on offer. These SSBNs were all manned by two crews, like the US Navy boats, to allow a very rapid turnaround between patrols.

In 1979, it was finally admitted that the British had developed their own 'semi-MIRV' warhead for Polaris, codenamed 'Chevaline'. Basically the A-3TK 'Chevaline' is a triple warhead capable of entering the target zone in a shallow trajectory to defeat ABM

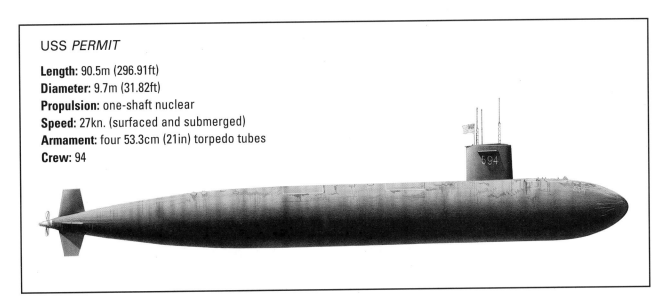

USS *PERMIT*

Length: 90.5m (296.91ft)
Diameter: 9.7m (31.82ft)
Propulsion: one-shaft nuclear
Speed: 27kn. (surfaced and submerged)
Armament: four 53.3cm (21in) torpedo tubes
Crew: 94

Above: The 'Thresher' class marked the end of the experimental phase of SSN development, as the US Navy exploited the potential of the S5W reactor and BQQ-2 sonar.

defences, but accurate enough to hit three targets up to 40 miles apart. The French SLBMs have also been upgraded over the years. Mainland China's People's Liberation Army-Navy (PLAN) also joined the 'SSBN club' in 1987, when No.406 joined the fleet. Codenamed 'Xia' by Western intelligence, she appears to be the only SSBN in service, and is similar to Western SSBNs, but armed with only 12 missiles.

Once the attack-submarine (SSN) prototypes had been evaluated, design could begin to settle down. For the US Navy the chance came with the four 'Skate' (SSN-578) class begun in 1955, but further orders were cancelled when it became clear that major improvements could be made.

THE 'TEARDROP' HULL

The catalyst was the experimental *Albacore* (AGSS-569), whose revolutionary 'teardrop' hull improved speed and manoeuvrability. She was designed purely for maximum underwater performance, with no concessions to surface performance, and her advanced silver-zinc batteries yielded a reputed 33 knots (the actual figure remains secret to this day). The cost of the battery was said to be so high that the US Treasury demanded the return of the silver recovered from old cells.

The six 'Skipjack' (SSN-585) class built in 1956–61 set a new standard, with an underwater speed of 30 knots, thanks to the 'teardrop' hull and the Westinghouse S5W reactor plant. On a surfaced

displacement of 3119 tonnes (3070 tons) they were the fastest submarines of their time, and the hull was adapted to create the 'George Washington' class SSBNs with minimum delay. Unlike the *Nautilus* and her successors, the 'Skipjack' power plant drove a single shaft, the natural consequence of the tapering *Albacore* hull form. The US Navy was now set on a clear course, and the 11 'Thresher' (SSN-593) or 'Permit' (SSN-594) class which followed, used the same S5W power plant, as did the 42 larger 'Sturgeon' (SSN-613) class. Although the 'Skipjack' design was not noted for its quietness its speed and manoeuvrability made it very suitable for submarine-versus-submarine tactics. There was nothing new about the idea of 'setting a thief to catch a thief', as the 'R' class had demonstrated in 1918 and a few encounters had proved in World War II, but the sensors and weapons of the day were not tailored to the mission. With the 'Skipjacks' and their successors, anti-submarine warfare became a prime requirement.

SUBMARINE VERSUS SUBMARINE

The submarine has some unique advantages when hunting its own kind. For one thing, it becomes its own variable-depth sonar, going through thermal layers as it pleases (most of the time). For another, it can go wherever its quarry goes. Against that, an SSN is, of course, a very expensive vessel to operate, and comparatively few can be built (even by the US Navy and the Soviet Navy during the Cold War). The SSN's size means that it cannot operate in shallow water, and PWR powerplants can never be shut down completely at sea, so some residual noise in inescapable. At full power the SSN is very noisy indeed, and it must slow

down to allow its sensors to function. High speed is a strategic advantage; an SSN can make a high-speed transit of thousands of kilometres, in total secrecy. This was done during the Falklands War, although rumours and disinformation about British SSNs in the South Atlantic misled the Argentine Navy into thinking that the SSNs were on station much earlier.

The sonars developed for SSNs in the 1960s differed greatly from the original medium-frequency active sets used during and after World War II. The fear of every submariner is that the 'pings' of an active sonar will alert the enemy and allow him to get in the first shot. Modern submarine sonars are therefore mainly low-frequency passive sets, and the active

Sonars need a combat system to process their inputs and display the data in a form useable by the command team. The command team then selects a course of action, and the combat system designates specific weapons.

WIRE-GUIDED TORPEDOES

In modern SSNs the main weapon remains the long-range heavyweight wire-guided torpedo, despite being invented over 125 years ago. Profiting by pioneer work done in Germany during World War II, modern heavyweights (ie, weapons designed to sink ships and other submarines) are wire-guided, allowing them to respond to commands from the fire control system linked with or integrated into the combat system. The two-way wire link pays out from a spool left inside the torpedo tube and from a similar spool in the tail-section of the torpedo, to reduce the risk of the wire kinking or breaking from uneven tension. As it is two-way the torpedo's own seeker head can be used as an offboard sensor to relay target-data back to the fire control system.

Wire-guidance has its disadvantages. A 10,000-m (32,808-ft) run at 30 knots, for example, takes 10 minutes, during which time the tube cannot be reloaded for a second shot. The risk of mutual interference means that most current weapon control systems are designed to control only two torpedoes at a time. The wire can kink or break, depriving the torpedoes of guidance, so modern weapons have the facility to go into 'autonomous' mode, homing on information acquired by the seeker head. The physical constraints imposed by the torpedo body prevent even the most sophisticated active or passive seeker from matching the performance of the submarine's sonar, so autonomous mode is only a second-best solution.

ANTI-SHIP MISSILES

A relative newcomer to submarine warfare is the underwater-launched anti-ship missile. These are either ejected from a torpedo tube (now generally described as launch tubes because of the choice of weapons) in a neutrally buoyant capsule or fired from a vertical launcher. When the missile comes to the surface it broaches at a preset angle, using stabilising fins, and the missile flies clear of the water and assumes a normal flight-profile. Currently submarines

element is used only to emit a 'single ping' for ranging purposes. Passive flank arrays are now the standard means of ranging. Other sonars include: mine-avoidance sets; short-range high-frequency sets to spot obstacles ahead of the boat; under-ice sonars; and even aft-looking sonars for use when operating near the surface.

launch two types: tactical anti-ship missiles such as the UGM-84 Sub Harpoon or the SM-39 version of Exocet; and cruise missiles such as the BGM-109 Tomahawk or the Russian S-10 *Granat* (designated the SS-N-21 'Sampson' by NATO but popularly known in the US Navy as the 'Tomahawkski').

'PICTURING' THE TARGET

Submarine fire control systems are intended to control specific weapons, but modern command systems must present a 'tactical picture' to the command team (usually the commanding officer and a team of operators) to show the position and identity of all contacts and to predict their movements. Data must be extracted from all the sonars (usually operating passively), but unlike radar, sonars are imprecise and slow. Nor is sonar the only source of data. Electronic support measures (ESM) provide analysis of above-water radio and radar transmissions, the periscope, and external intelligence through a satellite link all provide additional information to the command team. Strange as it may seem, a 'quick look' through the periscope is required by most submarine commanders to verify the tactical picture.

Modern periscopes are not simple: infrared sensors, laser rangefinders, low-light television cameras and thermal-imagers pass information directly to the combat system through a fibre-optic link. Determining the contact's location and direction of

Above: The *Rubis* (S601) was the first SSN built for the French Navy, and featured an unusually compact reactor plant. All four boats have been modernised.

movement may take some minutes, even hours. At times a contact may be detected, but not positively identified and tracked before it moves out of sonar range. Nor is the information extracted in a form which is easily interpreted; it must be manipulated and processed to produce a clear tactical picture. This is divided into three areas: track-management, target-motion analysis (TMA) and display-management.

SOVIET NAVY'S 'CHARLIE' SSGN

The Soviet Navy always feared the power of American carrier strikes against the heartland, and saw the long-range cruise missile as a counter. After the comparatively crude weapon systems designed for the 'Juliett' and 'Echo' classes, the designers produced the much more advanced Project 670 Skat ('Charlie') type. The P-20L missile (SS-N-7) could be fired submerged, using intermittent radar data, and although the 24-knot 'Charlie' was too slow to catch a carrier battle group, it was seen as a dangerous threat, able to slip inside the escort screen and give the defences as little time as possible to initiate counter-measures. The improved *Skat-M* ('Charlie II') had the P-120 *Malakhit* (SS-N-9 'Siren'), capable of a higher

launch-speed and having a range of 120km (66 miles). A 'Charlie I' was leased to India in 1988 for three years as INS *Chakra*, but the Indian Navy was not particularly happy with the result. According to reports, Indian personnel were never allowed to control the nuclear plant or become familiar with the missile control centre. Plans to lease a second 'Charlie' were dropped.

The 'Charlie' design appears to have been adapted as an SSGN from an earlier SSN proposal, which would account for its relatively unsatisfactory performance. The real successors to the 'Echo' appear to be the huge 12,700-tonne (12,500-ton) Project 949 Antey class, known in the West as 'Oscar'. They are armed with 12 P-500 *Granit* (SS-N-19 'Shipwreck') anti-ship missiles, which are guided by satellite data. The 'Oscar' class and its missiles are a formidable combination, and only the collapse of the Soviet Union slowed down the programme. The last six 'Oscar IIs' were broken up after 1992.

In parallel, the Soviet Navy was working on a major advance in submarine design. Soon after the commissioning of the first 'November' in August 1958, the designers were authorised to start work on a new high-speed boat and to develop the related technologies. Out of this, and after a long gestation, came Project 661, the *Anchar* or 'Papa'. The prototype was laid down at Severodvinsk in the Arctic at the end of 1963 and commissioned exactly six years later. She was armed with four 53.3cm (21in) torpedo-tubes and 12 torpedoes, and ten P-70 *Ametist* 60km (32.4 mile) cruise missiles. Driven by two reactors, two turbines and two shafts, the 80,000hp plant drove the *Anchar*, reaching 44.7 knots on trials, still a world record. Although displacing only 5283 tonnes (5200 tons) on the surface she could dive to 400m (1312.3ft), (100m [328.08ft] more than the 'November'), thanks to a novel titanium alloy hull.

THE ADVANTAGES OF TITANIUM

For Project 661 a new metallurgical division was created, producing plates, frames, and forgings in titanium. The advantages of the new material included lightness, strength, low corrosion and an absence of a magnetic signature, but the cost was unbearably high. The lengthy building time and the unreliability of the power plant also meant that Project 661 never went into series production.

The next titanium-hulled design was the Project 705 *Lira*, known in the West as the 'Alfa'. The prototype was built in Leningrad (now St Petersburg) and commissioned in December 1971. Five more followed in 1972–82. On a surfaced displacement of only 2337 tonnes (2300 tons) the *Lira* was armed with six 53.3cm (21in) torpedo tubes and 12 torpedoes. A single reactor and turbine plant drove the boat at 42 knots. American and British submariners were astounded when they encountered the 'Alfa' at sea, and the phenomenal speed and (exaggerated) deep-diving capability created something close to panic in the anti-submarine warfare community. Yet Western assessments of the 'Alfa' failed to take into account the serious fault which developed in the 40,000hp plant's lead-bismuth (Pb-Bi) cooling. The plant was very unreliable and the cost led to the Lira being nicknamed the 'Golden Fish'. Nor had the design stressed deep diving – an overestimate which resulted in massive investment in the West to create deep-running torpedoes.

Full exploitation of the new technology was finally achieved in the Project 685 *Plavnik* or 'Mike' prototype *Komsomolets* (*K.278*), built at Severodvinsk in 1978–83. Her titanium hull allowed diving down to 546.75 fathoms, but the 40,000hp reactor plant produced a more modest 30 knots. Armament was six launch tubes and 28 torpedoes and missiles. This remarkable submarine was tragically lost in the Barents Sea in 1989 after a fire in the reactor compartment.

Series production was achieved once more with the Project 945 'Sierra' design. The choice of the Krasnoe Sormovo inland shipyard at Nizhny Novgorod put an upper limit on size, but in spite of this factor, weapon-load, was increased to 40 torpedoes and missiles. Although a total of 40 boats was planned only two 'Sierra Is' and two 'Sierra IIs' came into service between 1984 and 1993. The internal problems of the Soviet economy were beginning to show, and the military's huge demands for money could no longer be met.

OTHER SOVIET IMPROVEMENTS

Steel construction did not stop when the titanium-hulled boats were under construction. The Project 671 *Ersh* ('Victor') series first appeared in 1967, a 4369-tonne (4300-ton) boat with many American features, notably a 'teardrop' hull and a single propeller shaft. A 30,000hp reactor plant (twice the power of the S5W) drove the boat at 30 knots, and armament was 18 torpedoes and RPK-2 *Viyoga* (SS-N-15 'Starfish') anti-submarine missiles. These impressive SSNs were followed by the Project 671RT 'Victor II' and the

Right: 'Los Angeles' class SSNs, like the *Buffalo* here, have high-speed performance at the expense of deep diving, and are the most numerous class of SSNs ever built.

Project 671RTM *Shchuka* 'Victor III' with a significantly improved combat system. The improvement in efficiency led some in the West to suspect that the Soviets had obtained Western technology. It was also clear that the Soviets had finally realised that their noisy submarines were being tracked with ease by Western passive sonars, and a big effort was made to silence machinery and to improve hull design. The 'Victor III' was also armed with four 65cm (25.6in) launch tubes for the RPK-6 *Vodopod* (SS-N-16 'Stallion') anti-submarine missile system.

The successor to the 'Victor' design is the Project 971 *Bars*, known to the West as the 'Akula'. Intended to complement the 'Sierra', it is meant primarily as a launch-platform for the S-10 Granat cruise missile. Armament of the 'Akula I' includes only two 53.3cm (21in) tubes for torpedoes and six 65cm (25.6in) tubes for missiles. The 'Akula II' has six external tubes to increase firepower.

In 1970, the first of a series of 10,160-tonne (10,000-ton) SSBNs was started at Severodvinsk – the Project 667 *Murena* ('Delta'). The final variant, Project 667 BDRM *Delfin*, was armed with 16 R29RM *Shtil* (SS-N-23 'Skiff'), a three-stage liquid-fuelled missile credited with a range of 8300km (4469 miles). In 1983, the first Project 941 *Akula* ('Typhoon') SSBN appeared, a colossal 18,797-tonne (18,500-ton) boat armed with 24 R-39 *Taifun* (SS-N-20 'Sturgeon') missiles. Unlike the 'Delta' and older SSBNs, the six 'Typhoons' were intended to spend up to a year on the seabed, surviving a nuclear exchange to make a 'second strike'.

THE WEST HARNESSES ITS RESOURCES

The effect on the West of all these advances was not meek submissiveness, but a determination to harness its superior technical and industrial resources. The US Navy embarked on a huge construction programme, building an eventual total of 62 'Los Angeles' (SSN-688) class SSNs between 1972 and 1995, and a new-generation SSBN, the 'Ohio' (SSBN-726) class, armed with the C4 Trident I missile, with a range of 7408km (4000 miles). In time the Trident I was replaced by the D5 Trident II, with a range of 11,112km (6000 mile), but the four oldest boats will not be upgraded to launch the larger Trident II.

These technical developments were mirrored elsewhere in the West. For example, the Royal Navy had bought an S5W reactor for its first SSN – HMS *Dreadnought* – in 1958, and since then it had developed its own reactor design for five SSNs and four SSBNs. The first series-production design was the *Swiftsure*, a 4470-tonne (4400-ton) boat driven by a PWR 1 reactor plant at 30 knots, and armed with five tubes. The hull-form was slightly modified for the

4775-tonne (4700-ton) 'Trafalgar' class, with similar performance but with improved systems.

NUCLEAR SUBMARINES AT WAR

Ironically the Royal Navy was the first to use nuclear submarines in a war situation. In 1982, British SSNs were the first to be sent to the South Atlantic when Argentina invaded the Falkland Islands. Their primary role was reconnaissance, and while the task force steamed south the SSNs tailed Argentine surface units, particularly the carrier ARA *Veinticinco de Mayo*. Three of the British SSNs were fitted hurriedly with a US Navy passive detection device to detect Argentine radio and radar transmissions. When radio traffic indicated the launch of an air strike the SSN was able to transmit a warning to the task force commander via a satellite link, in time to alert the combat air patrol.

As part of their overall strategy the Royal Navy had declared a Total Exclusion Zone around the Falkland Islands, and had warned the Argentine Government that any of their forces found to be operating outside Argentine territorial waters (author's emphasis) would be liable to attack. Despite this the Argentine Navy had launched a three-pronged movement, intended to lure the British into action on terms favourable to itself. Throughout the day on 1 May, the cruiser *General Belgrano* and her escorting destroyers had been patrolling to the southwest, while to the northwest the *Veinticinco de Mayo* was preparing to launch an air strike. Both these forces were being shadowed by British SSNs, and clearly both posed a threat – the cruiser and her escort with their guns and Exocet anti-ship missiles, and the carrier with her air group.

SINKING THE *BELGRANO*

By dawn on 2 May the carrier was 370.4km (about 200 miles) away from the British carriers, and ready to launch her aircraft, but there was insufficient wind over the deck, and the operation was cancelled. The *General Belgrano* was not to know that HMS *Conqueror* was maintaining discreet surveillance at a range of 370.4km (about 200 miles), using the (then) highly secret 2026 towed sonar array. Although the old cruiser, a veteran of Pearl Harbor, was roughly 36 miles outside the Total Exclusion Zone she was thought to pose a serious threat to British light forces

Below: The Project 705 SSNs were unique, being designed for high-speed interception. The titanium hull and light reactor shielding gave very high speed.

in the area, and HMS *Conqueror* was given permission to sink her. Three straight-running Mk 8 torpedoes hit the *General Belgrano*, blowing off her bow and holing her engine room. She sank in heavy weather while her two escorts pursued the *Conqueror* for two hours in a vain attempt to sink her. In the heavy seas, approximately 370 of her crew of over 1000 drowned or died of exposure.

The subsequent criticism of the sinking focused on the argument that the cruiser was 'heading for home', and that the sinking was a brutal way of terminating peace negotiations. In fact the British Chief of the Defence Staff, Admiral Lewin, later admitted that the *Veinticinco de Mayo* could have been sunk by her shadower, but the *General Belgrano* was chosen instead because the loss of the Armada Republica, Argentina's most prestigious unit, might have been seen as 'overkill'. As for the charge that the *General Belgrano* was heading away from the Total Exclusion Zone, Argentine warships were already liable to be attacked outside 22.2km (12 miles) from the coast of Argentina. A senior ARA flag-officer later said publicly that he would have given the same order, if roles had been reversed.

THE GULF WAR

The other use of nuclear submarines in war was during the Gulf War in 1991, when no fewer than 18 US Navy SSNs were used for reconnaissance and surveillance. One, the USS *Louisville* (SSN-724) launched Tomahawk cruise missiles from the Red Sea, while her sister *Pittsburgh* (SSN-720) launched Tomahawks from the Eastern Mediterranean. Their task was to roll up the flanks of Iraq's air defence

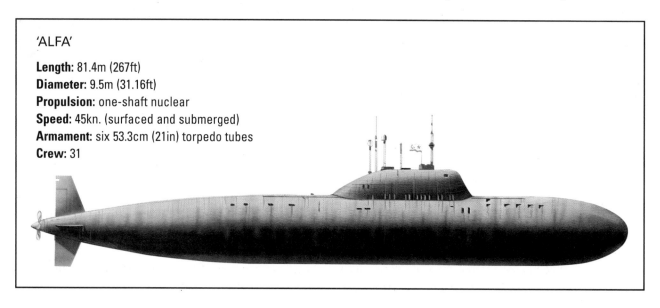

'ALFA'

Length: 81.4m (267ft)
Diameter: 9.5m (31.16ft)
Propulsion: one-shaft nuclear
Speed: 45kn. (surfaced and submerged)
Armament: six 53.3cm (21in) torpedo tubes
Crew: 31

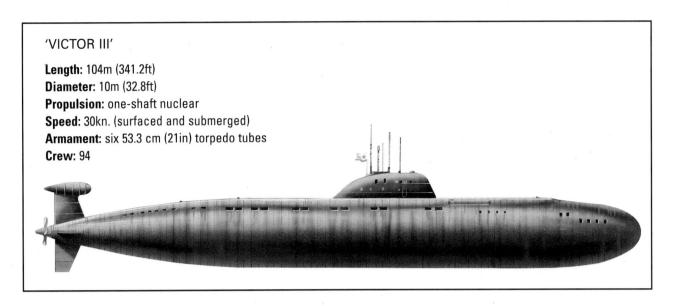

'VICTOR III'

Length: 104m (341.2ft)
Diameter: 10m (32.8ft)
Propulsion: one-shaft nuclear
Speed: 30kn. (surfaced and submerged)
Armament: six 53.3 cm (21in) torpedo tubes
Crew: 94

Above: The most distinctive feature of the Russian 'Victor III' nuclear attack submarine is the teardrop-shaped pod on top of the upper rudder housing a towed array sonar.

system by knocking out crucial power stations and communications centres, sharing the task with surface ships.

OTHER NUCLEAR-ARMED NAVIES

The French Navy authorised its first SSNs under the *Sousmarin Nuclèaire de Chasse* project in 1964, but it was cancelled four years later, only to be reinstated as the *Sousmarin Nuclèaire Attaque* 1972 (SNA 72). This finally materialised as the 'Rubis' class of four units, built in 1976–88. These were the smallest operational SSNs in any navy, as a result of the small volume of the CAS 48 reactor plant, but they were intended only for anti-surface warfare, and were very noisy. Silencing measures were applied to the next batch of four, the 'Amethyste' class; the name coincided with the acronym for *Amelioration Tactique Hydrodynamique Silence Transmission Ecoute*. These measures proved sufficiently effective, and the four 'Rubis' class were brought to the same standard.

The French also needed to replace their old SSBNs, but unlike the British, they continued to insist on developing an all-French SLBM system. The new *Triomphant* is in service, and is armed with the M4 missile, and her sister *Temeraire* is under construction at Cherbourg. The M5 follow-on missile has been cancelled but the upgraded M45 will arm future SSBNs and the upgraded *Triomphant* and *Temeraire*. The SSBNs are specifically exempt from defence budget cuts, which have accounted for the last two 'Amethyste'

class SSNs. Plans have been announced for a future SSN, but this will not happen until the next century.

Rumours of a new Chinese SSN to follow the 'Han' class are common, but no confirmation has been seen publicly. Although the Indian and Brazilian Navies continue to talk of building SSNs the cost is resulting in a length gestation.

THE COST OF DECOMMISSIONING

Other navies have long since abandoned hope of joining the nuclear club. The true cost of decommissioning nuclear-powered ships is now all too obvious. The Russian Navy gave up on the problem entirely, dumping retired SSNs and SSBNs and even dumping the reactors in deep water. Today, the Russians admit there are 52 assorted nuclear submarines lying derelict off the submarine base at Murmansk, and a consortium of American and Norwegian specialists has been awarded a contract to render these wrecks less harmful. Even the US Navy cannot afford to recore its nuclear reactors, and several SSNs have been taken out of commission early. The problem is the reactor core, which remains radioactive for many years after the reactor plant has been cooled down. For the Russians the problem is exacerbated by the lead-bismuth cooling systems in some of their boats. When the coolant is allowed to cool (usually because the Russian Navy cannot afford to pay its electricity bills), the reactor becomes very difficult to dismantle. Experts say that the safest way to dispose of radioactive cores is to drop them in the deepest part of the ocean, but environmentalists have objected fiercely, and landfill sites are the only alternative. Admiral Rickover's dream of an all-nuclear navy has faded, and his successors have inherited an intractable problem.

CHAPTER FIVE

The SSK Makes a Comeback

Although the nuclear-powered submarine (SSN) threatened to make the diesel-electric submarine obsolete, the high cost of nuclear power deterred many navies from adopting it. Instead, the 'conventional' submarine (SSK) developed its own unique qualities of quietness and shallow-water performance to offset the advantages of the SSN.

With the advent of the *Nautilus* and the 'November' class SSNs, many assumed that the age of the 'conventional' diesel-electric submarine was about to end. Indeed, some began to talk of 'true submarines' and mere 'submersibles', reviving the old French term to suggest inferior status. On paper the SSN's huge advantages in speed and submerged endurance could never be matched by the conventional boat (SS in US Navy parlance), not even the

Left: The German Navy's new Type 212 is one of the most advanced non-nuclear submarine designs in the world. It uses fuel cells to extend underwater endurance.

latest 'hunter-killers' (SSKs, as all SSs are now known). Yet, 40 years later more SSKs are being built than ever before. What went wrong?

As shown in the previous chapter, the nuclear submarine has proved much more expensive than its advocates claimed, not just in acquisition but in through-life cost and, now, in the final years of the century, in disposal costs. The SSK, on the other hand, has nearly as much deterrent value as the SSN, is armed with the same weapons, has lower through-life costs, virtually no hidden disposal costs, and can perform specialised tasks denied to SSNs. But SSKs are not cheap; they impose heavy burdens on small

Above: The USS *Gudgeon* was one of six 'Tang' class submarines built in 1949–52 to incorporate lessons learned in wartime, especially from Germany's XXI boats.

navies in terms of specialist personnel and shoreside support. But they are seen by many navies as prestigious, and the market for them is expanding rapidly.

The US Navy became so dominated by the nuclear lobby that it built its last SSKs, the three 'Barbel' (SS-580) class in the late 1950s. They were very impressive, 2174 tonnes (2140 tons) on the surface and capable of 21 knots in short bursts. They were also the first to have all controls centralised in an 'attack centre'. The GUPPY III programme recently had been initiated: nine GUPPY IIs lengthened by 3.05m (10ft) to provide a longer control room and a larger sail. An updated fire control system allowed them to fire the Mk 45 ASTOR nuclear anti-submarine torpedo. This fearsome weapon was credited with a kill probability of 2 – 'Him and Me', because its blast radius exceeded its range. The 'Tang' (SS-563) and 'Darter' (SS-576) classes commissioned in the 1950s were an attempt to assimilate the lessons of the German Type

XXI design. Unfortunately the advanced Fairbanks Morse 'pancake' radial diesel was not successful, and they were re-engined with conventional machinery.

The Soviet Navy never lost faith in the SSK, and continued to build them in parallel with SSNs. When the huge Project 613 'Whiskey' programme came to an end in 1958 no fewer than 215 had been built, and 21 more were assembled in Chinese yards. The improved Project 633 'Romeo' type never achieved the same popularity – 20 being built in 1956–64 for the Soviet Navy and others built for export. The Project 611 'Zulu' type, a 1930.5-tonne (1900-ton) ocean-going boat, ran to 30 units, but large-scale production returned with the 62 Project 641 'Foxtrots' built from the early 1960s to 1971. The 19 Project 641 BUKI 'Som' class ('Tango') were specialised anti-submarine boats built from 'Foxtrot' components.

RUSSIA'S GREATEST SUCCESS – THE 'KILO'

This huge force of conventional submarines hypnotised Western analysts, who gullibly accepted Soviet claims that all were kept in a high state of readiness. In fact the majority were kept as a 'material reserve',

some without engines and other essential equipment. The Soviet command economy relied on lengthy production runs to keep the shipyards busy, and if a submarine was lost or a transfer to a friendly navy was required, replacement hulls could be brought forward from reserve. In fact, many were given to satellite countries in the Third World, where they tended to become permanent features of the dockyards.

The Russians' greatest success has been the 2337-tonne (2300-ton) Project 877 design, designated the 'Kilo' by Western intelligence. Designed by the Rubin Bureau (formerly TsKB-18) to a staff requirement issued in 1974, the design split into two parallel projects – the Granay for the Soviet Navy and the Warshavyanka for export. The first boat, built at the Komsomolsk yard on the Amur River in the Far East, was launched in September 1980 and entered service 18 months later. Production lines were also set up at Gorkiy (now Nizhny Novgorod) and Leningrad (now St Petersburg), but construction is now concentrated at the Admiralty Shipyard in St Petersburg.

Project 877 was designed to exploit the new 'Second Captain' concept, in which a single central computer performs both fire control and ship control functions automatically. Most functions are controlled from a central panel, with fire control data entered automatically for the first time, and diving and machinery control and even weapon-loading automated. This is now common in Western submarines, but it was a major technology step for the Russians, and the crew of 52 is small for such a big SSK. An Albacore was adopted, with raft-mounted main and auxiliary machinery. Unlike earlier Soviet SSKs, the design emphasises underwater performance.

In its basic form Project 877 has four internal reloadable torpedo tubes and two external tubes. The Project 877E variant, intended for export, has six internal 533mm (20.86in) launch tubes, but cannot fire wire-guided torpedoes. Project 877M for the Soviet Navy has only four internal tubes, but all capable of firing wire-guided torpedoes. Project 877EM has six internal tubes, two of them for wire-guided torpedoes, and the family has since been extended to incorporate a new combat system and other improvements. Project 636 differs in being slightly longer, and has a more powerful air-conditioning plant and better accommodation to appeal to Middle East and Far East customers. Including allies, the Project 877 has been supplied to six navies, and the total built is 24 for the Soviet/Russian Navy and 18 exported.

Below: A Soviet Project 641 BUKI 'Tango' class SSK off the Shetlands in June 1985. They were improvised from 'Foxtrot' components and surplus 'Juliett' hulls.

The Project 1650 design is believed to be a scaled-down version of the 'Kilo', also from Rubin, with the Amur variant intended for the Russian Navy and the Lada for export. Two were reported in the Russian press as being laid down by the Admiralty Shipyard in December 1997 – one for the Russian Navy and one for an unidentified foreign customer. The cost was quoted at about US$300 million each, with delivery planned for 2000–1. American sources say Project 1650 displaces no more than 1422 tonnes (1400 tons) on the surface and takes automation even further than Project 877. The diesel is said to drive an AC generator, which charges the battery through a solid-state converter, a very compact propulsion plant. Armament is six tubes and 18 torpedoes, and the crew is no more than 45.

OTHER NAVIES

The Chinese PLAN was encouraged to build up its SSK strength, at first by the supply of material for assembly locally, and then by handing over plans of the 'Romeo'. China in turn helped the Democratic People's Republic of Korea to establish a submarine force.

The Royal Navy developed a successful series of submarines from the 1950s – the 'Porpoise' class and the similar but improved 'Oberon' class. The 'Oberon' design was in its day highly successful, and was exported to Australia, Brazil, Canada and Chile.

Its most striking attribute was its silent running, and the Royal Navy did not discard its 13 boats until the early 1990s. Britain's major rival as a submarine exporter was France, which sold the smaller 'Daphne' design to Pakistan, Portugal, South Africa and Spain. Since then the French Navy's 'Agosta' design has been sold to Pakistan and Spain.

The Indian Navy turned to the Soviet Union in the 1960s when it started its submarine service. Eight Project 641 'Foxtrot' type SSKs were acquired in 1970–74, conferring on India the status of a regional superpower. They were supplemented by four IKL Type 1500 boats from the early 1980s – two built by HDW at Kiel and two built at Bombay by Mazagon Dock as the 'Shishumar' class. The programme suffered major delays because of the lack of indigenous industrial capabilty, which condemned HDW to import virtually all materials. The lack of local expertise also caused length delays; the *Shalki* took eight years to build, and as a result the programme was stopped. Instead, nine Project 877EM 'Kilo' type 'Sindhugosh' class SSKs have been bought from Russia since the mid-1980s, with a tenth still to be delivered. The latest, the *Sindhurakshak*, was on her way to India from the Baltic in January 1998.

India's rival, neighbouring Pakistan, has always been overshadowed, but her small navy has worked

Left: HMS *Sealion*, one of eight 'Porpoise' class SSKs built in the 1950s to incorporate Type XXI ideas and war lessons. They were armed with Mk 8 and Mk 20 torpedoes.

Below: The French SSK *La Praya* is one of four 'Agosta' class boats built in the 1970s. The design has been exported to Spain and Pakistan, with minor improvements.

hard to keep pace with New Delhi's ambitious plans. In 1964, the US Navy transferred the ex-'Tench' class *Diabolo* (SS-479) for training, and in 1967 the first of four 'Daphne' class SSKs were ordered in France. The lead-boat, PNS *Hangor*, soon justified her existence, for the Indo-Pakistan War broke out the year after she was commissioned. She sank the Indian frigate *Khukri* with a torpedo on 9 December 1971, but the *Ghazi* had already been sunk by Indian escorts while she was trying to torpedo the aircraft carrier INS *Vikrant* at the start of the war.

In 1975 a replacement 'Daphne', the *Cachalote*, was bought from the cash-strapped Portuguese Navy and renamed *Ghazi*. When three years later France enforced a United Nations embargo and refused to deliver two 'Agosta' class to South Africa, Pakistan very promptly took over the contract. They were renamed *Hashmat* (ex-SAS *Astrant*) and *Hurmat* (ex-SAS *Adventurous*). Although nominally similar, the three Agosta-90B type ordered in France in 1994 have many differences, not least greater diving depth through the use of improved steel, and the modern SUBTICS combat system. The first boat was laid down

Below: The Pakistani *Hurmat* (S-136) is one of a pair of French 'Agosta' class SSKs built for South Africa in the 1970s, which were embargoed and then sold in Asia.

at Cherbourg in 1995 for delivery in 1999, while material for the second was shipped to Karachi for assembly under French supervision. The third boat is to have an eight-metre (26.24-ft) 'plug' inserted, housing a 200kW MESMA air-independent propulsion (AIP) system, and the earlier boats will be modified to the same standard. These submarines will also be the first non-French boats to be armed with the French SM-39 Exocet missile, as well as F-17 Mod 2 torpedoes.

Subject to strict tonnage limits, the newly created West German *Bundesmarine* was permitted to establish a submarine force from 1955. The first steps were slow, the raising of two Type XXIII coastal U-boats and a Type XXI. These were repaired and put back into service as the *Hai* and *Hecht* (Type 240) and *Wilhelm Bauer* (Type 241), before design work started on the 406-tonne (400-ton) Type 201 and the even smaller 101.6-tonne (100-ton) Type 201. The work was entrusted to *Ingenieurkontor Lübeck* (IKL) a design bureau founded by the former U-boat designer Dr Ulrich Gabler. The 406-tonne (400-ton) Type 205 boats (*U.1–2* and *U.4–12*) were the first operational submarines in the Federal German Navy, and they were followed by the 18 Type 206 (*U.13–30*). Building on this experience IKL was able to export the Type 205 to Denmark and the Type 207 to Norway, but the bureau's greatest success was the Type 209 series. From the

Above: An unidentified IKL Type 209/1200 SSK on trials. This small design has proved an outstanding export success, and is still in production in South Korea.

early 1970s these 1117–1422-tonne (1100–1400-ton) boats were built for Argentina, Brazil, Chile, Colombia, Ecuador, Greece, Indonesia, Peru, South Korea, Turkey and Venezuela. An enlarged Type 1500 design was sold to India as the 'Shishumar' class. These boats were all built by HDW at Kiel, but the *Bundesmarine* orders were shared with Thyssen Nordseewerke (TNSW) at Emden, who succeeded in selling its TR 1700 design to Argentina in the late 1970s.

ARGENTINA AND THE FALKLANDS WAR

Argentina, like its rivals Brazil and Chile, had operated submarines before World War II, but when the Falklands War broke out in April 1982 the force included one seaworthy ex-Balao, the *Santa Fé* (ex-

USS *Catfish*), her unseaworthy sister *Santiago del Estero* (ex-USS *Chivo*), and one of a pair of Type 209/1200 boats built in Argentina with technical assistance from HDW.

The *Santa Fé* was an early casualty, being caught on the surface by British naval helicopters on 25 April 1982. She was attempting to run ammunition and supplies to the small garrison on the island of South Georgia when she was crippled by hits from AS 12 antitank missiles. After being beached the crew surrendered. Her gutted sister played a passive role, being

towed from place to place in the hope that the British would assume she was in commission. Only one Type 209 boat, the *San Luis*, was seaworthy, as her sister *Salta* was soon out of action with engine trouble.

Although many claims were made for the performance of the *San Luis* after the war, mainly to the effect that she had penetrated the anti-submarine screen of the British task force with ease, and had only been robbed of success because of torpedo failures or maintenance problems affecting her combat system. The reaction by the German torpedo-manufacturers was understandable; any suggestion that their weapons were 'duds' was bad for business. The claims of up to three hits on the carrier HMS *Invincible* do not hold water; not even Captain Azcueta of the *San Luis* claimed to have sighted a carrier. He claimed to have fired only three torpedoes in all, two SUT heavyweights, one each against a destroyer or frigate, and a Mk 37 against a submarine, none of which hit. The explanation is quite prosaic; the Argentine Navy was overawed by the Royal Navy's reputation as a specialist anti-submarine force, and the *San Luis* fired her torpedoes at too great a distance (in excess of 8000m [26,246.7ft]), using only passive bearings to estimate the range.

THE MARKET FOR SSKS

Proliferation was also promoted by the transfer of a number of overage American submarines to friendly countries, mostly GUPPY II variants and latterly GUPPY IIIs and Tangs. But the supply of elderly

Below: To avoid upsetting the Arab world, IKL and HDW negotiated a licence agreement with Vickers to build a Type 540 variant of the Type 206 for the Israeli Navy.

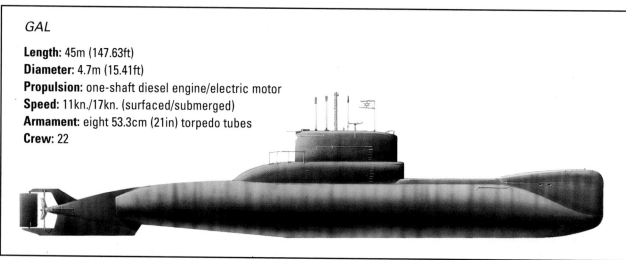

GAL

Length: 45m (147.63ft)
Diameter: 4.7m (15.41ft)
Propulsion: one-shaft diesel engine/electric motor
Speed: 11kn./17kn. (surfaced/submerged)
Armament: eight 53.3cm (21in) torpedo tubes
Crew: 22

Above: The German Navy built 18 Type 106 SSKs in the 1970s, of which 12 modernised Type 206As survive. The 'S' pennant number bears no relation to the hull number.

submarines eventually dried up, and as Britain and France followed the American lead in devoting ever-greater resources to SSNs and SSBNs, customers began to look elsewhere for SSKs. In a bid to under-cut European suppliers the Chinese took to offering 'Romeos' at so-called 'friendship prices', but the only customer for these obsolescent boats was Egypt, which bought four in the early 1980s. But Europe remained the main source, with SSKs in service in the Royal Navy, as well as the Danish, Dutch, French, German, Greek, Italian, Norwegian, Swedish, Turkish and Yugoslavian navies.

The Dutch scored an early success, selling two 'Hai Lung' class to the Republic of China (Taiwan), but when *Rotterdamsche Droogdok Maatschappij* (RDM)

was approached to build two more of its 'Moray' design, the People's Republic put heavy diplomatic pressure on the Netherlands Government to stop the sale. Similar arm-twisting was used to stop HDW from selling IKL Type 209 boats to Taiwan recently. Such is the fear of losing Chinese trade that all governments have so far refused to allow their shipyards to accept a contract from Taiwan, despite its support from the United States as an anti-Communist state.

The Spanish Navy has a long association with submarines, dating back to Narciso Montjuriol and

Isaac Peral in the 19th century, but the ravages of the Civil War all but destroyed the industrial base which had provided indigenous submarines. Under the Mutual Defence Aid Programme the US Department of Defense transferred the ex-'Balao' class *Kraken* (SS-370) in 1959, and she served as the *Almirante Garcia de los Reyes* for another 23 years. In 1971–74 four more GUPPY IIA 'Balao' class were transferred: *Cosme Garcia* (ex-USS *Bang*), *Isaac Peral* (ex-USS *Ronquil*), *Narciso Montjuriol (i)* (ex-USS *Picuda*) and *Narciso Montjuriol (ii)* (ex-USS *Jallao*). The duplication of names happened because the first *Narciso Montjuriol* developed machinery defects and had to be replaced.

TECHNOLOGY-TRANSFER AGREEMENTS

A technology-transfer agreement was signed with France in 1966 to re-create a submarine-building capability, and the result was four Daphné type, known as the 'Delfin' class, built at Cartagena in 1968–73 with French technical assistance. In 1977–86 Cartagena built four Agosta type, the 'Galerna' class. The French hoped to win another contract, but uncertainty about future submarine strength and a shortage of funds has allowed the Spanish Navy to defer a decision. Instead, state shipbuilders *Empresa Nacional Bazan* and DCN in France agreed to work together to develop an export

design. This is the 2032-tonne (2000-ton) 'Scorpäne', in which the partners have a 40 : 60 share. Late in 1997, after lengthy negotiations, the Chilean Navy agreed to buy two 'Scorpänes' to replace its elderly British-built 'Oberon' types *O'Brien* and *Hyatt*. Full details have not yet been released, but the electronics will be a mixture of German (sonars) and French (SUBTICS combat system). The decision is a blow for the German Submarine Consortium, which hoped to provide two more Type 209s to match the existing Type 209/1300 boats *Thomson* and *Simpson*.

When HDW scored its string of successes with the IKL Type 209 designs, many of its customers bought only two boats. In practice this is inadequate if the navy is serious about getting its submarines to sea regularly. The refit cycle becomes so tight that it is impossible to guarantee even one ready to go to sea. Even three boats is too few, as the South African Navy found with its French-built 'Daphné type. Four is adequate, five is better and six is ideal. Most of the navies with two submarines have since had second thoughts, and have sought to buy more.

Below: The Indian Navy ordered two IKL Type 1500 SSKs from HDW in Germany in 1981. The models marked the final evolution to the Type 209 design.

Above: SAS *Maria van Riebeeck* is one of three 'Daphné' type SSKs built in France in 1968–71. They have been extensively modernised, including refurbished torpedoes.

The German Submarine Consortium (containing IKL, HDW, TNSW and the major equipment suppliers) thought it had won the long battle to sell two more Type 209 boats to Indonesia. Then, in 1997, out of the blue, the decision was made to buy five redundant Type 206 boats from the German Navy, but the financial crisis which wrecked the Indonesian economy has resulted in cancellation of that deal. The same submarines had been offered to Singapore as part of a package, the Type 206 boats to be used for interim training until new construction was ready. In 1996, however, the Republic of Singapore Navy bought a second-hand submarine, the *Sjobjornen* ('Sea Bear') from the Royal Swedish Navy, followed by three of her sisters.

South Korea also wanted a submarine force, but the Ministry of National Defence did not bother with an interim purchase for training, and ordered nine Type 209 boats from HDW. The first was built at Kiel but the remainder have been built by Daewoo Heavy Industries at Okpo. The Ministry has recently signed a technology-transfer agreement with HDW to allow Daewoo to build the next generation of SSKs, a 3048-tonne (3000-ton) ocean-going design, possibly with an AIP system.

JAPAN'S SUPERIOR FLEET

Japan's Maritime Self Defence Force (MSDF) has one of the best-equipped and largest submarine forces in the Pacific. When it was created in the mid-1950s the US Navy lent the 13-year-old 'Gato' class boat *Mingo* (SS-261), and she was renamed the *Kuroshio* (SS-501). Her role was to train a new generation of submarine specialists, but by the time she was returned to the US Navy the MSDF's first indigenous design, the *Oyashio* (SS-511) had been built by Kawasaki Heavy Industries at Kobe. Apart from her schnorkel, the design was modest, with only four torpedo tubes on a submerged displacement of 1422 tonnes (1400 tons). Four even smaller submarines followed, the 'Hayashio' (SS-521) and 'Natsushio' (SS-523) classes, displacing 914 tonnes (900 tons) submerged and armed with only three torpedo tubes.

The first large submarines were not built until the 1960s, the *Oshio* (SS-561), armed with six bow torpedo tubes and two stern tubes. Technical assistance from the US Navy resulted in a new design in the late 1970s, with a 'tear-drop' hull and many features of the Barbel design. These were the seven 'Uzushio' (SS-566) class, with diving planes on the sail, a diving depth of 200m (656ft), a separate emergency high-pressure blowing system and three-dimensional automatic steering. The next class, the

THE SSK MAKES A COMEBACK

Above: Two Type 206A submarines at Kiel in 1995. Some 18 were built in 1971–74 and armed with DM2A1 Seeschlange wire-guided torpedoes, plus DBQS-21D sonar in the bow.

2286-tonne (2250-ton) (surfaced) 'Yushio' (SS-573) class, were similar, but improved steel increased diving depth to 275m (902ft). The MSDF operates a 'scrap-and-build' policy, reducing older boats to training duties as their replacements come forward from the shipyards. This has the benefit of keeping the average age of hulls down (an important consideration for submarines), but retaining a relatively modern reserve force for recommissioning in the event of a national emergency.

The current 'Harushio' (SS-583) class are among the most powerful SSKs in the world, armed with Sub Harpoon missiles, 12 Japanese Type 89 heavyweight torpedoes and eight Type 80 lightweights for use against submarine targets. The latest boat, the

Oyashio (SS-590), displaces 3048 tonnes (3000 tons) submerged and her hull form shows that the basic Barbel ideas have been abandoned.

PROBLEMS FOR THE CHINESE NAVY

For many years the Chinese PLAN has operated a large fleet of SSKs, starting with a number of 'M' class, 'Shch' class, 'Whiskey' class and 'Romeo' class, but like the Soviet Navy, a big percentage of these were never in full commission. Chinese shipyards started to build 'Romeos' in the 1960s, and as late as 1995 a total of 70 was still listed. A derivative known to Western intelligence as the 'Ming' (Project 035) was started in the 1970s, and since then an improved variant has been built with German machinery and French fire control. In 1994–5 a new design, the Project 039 'Song' prototype started a lengthy series of sea trials. Chinese reports claimed that the SSK is armed with 'submarine-launched

cruise missiles', believed to be a tube-launched variant of the Ying-ji 8-2 anti-ship missile. In the summer of 1997 the SSK was still not operational, and production of the 'Ming' was continuing, suggesting that the PLAN wishes to be certain that the new SSK is fully proven before it goes into series production.

Many of the Chinese PLAN's problems had been caused by the breach with the Soviet Union in the 1960s, but relations have improved to such an extent that the PLAN has now bought Project 877 'Kilo' type SSKs and the improved Project 636 type. An order for two Project 877 EKM boats was placed in mid-1993, and the first was delivered from the Baltic in February 1995. The second arrived nine months later.

Reports suggest that these two SSKs were originally ordered by a Warsaw Pact Navy – either Poland or the former East German Democratic People's Republic. The next pair were, however, newly built Project 636, the 'westernised' export variant of the Project 877. The first was handed over to the PLAN in November 1997, with the second to follow in 1998. These four SSKs mark a major improvement for the PLAN, which has wasted its resources for years on producing obsolescent designs. The big

question which everyone now asks is, will Project 636 SSKs be built under licence in Chinese shipyards?

THE GERMAN NAVY

In July 1994 the German Navy finally ordered four Type 212 SSKs, a modest start to replacing the dozen Type 296A boats. The defence budget has been under intense pressure since the end of the Cold War, and the high cost of the Type 212 means that funding for any follow-on orders will be much later than hoped. The Navy was, however, not prepared to compromise on its desire for a state-of-the-art submarine. The ARGE group, which included HDW and TNSW, was given the demanding task of incorporating AIP as well as low-magnetic and acoustic signatures, and a range of advanced technologies.

The result is a submarine displacing 1829 tonnes (1800 tons) submerged, driven by an MTU diesel and a permanent-magnet motor at a maximum underwater speed of 20 knots. Armament includes six launch

Below: The Royal Netherlands Navy was given details of the US Navy's 'Barbel' class when ordering the *Zwaardvis* (seen here in August 1995) and *Zeeleeuw*.

ZEELEEUW

Length: 67.7m (222.11ft)
Diameter: 8.4m (27.55ft)
Propulsion: one-shaft diesel engines/electric motor
Speed: 13kn./20kn. (surfaced/submerged)
Armament: four 53.3cm (21in) torpedo tube,
   Sub Harpoon anti-ship missiles
Crew: 52

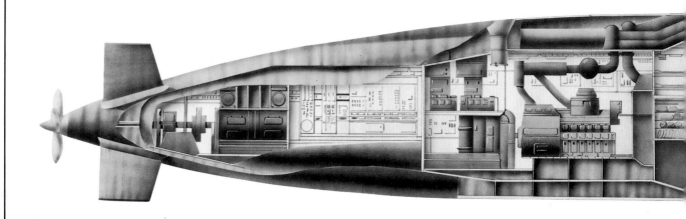

Above: The Royal Netherlands Navy's latest submarine design, the 'Walrus' class. The *Zeeleeuw* and her three sisters are armed with torpedoes and missiles.

tubes for DM2A4 Seehecht heavyweight torpedoes (18 reloads) and an optional load of mines, using an external 'belt'. Like earlier German SSKs the hull is fabricated of austenitic steel to reduce the risk of setting off magnetic mines. The design is to be adapted to meet the Italian Navy's needs (principally replacing the Norwegian MSI-90U combat system with an Italian equivalent). Many features have been incorporated into the Israeli 'Dolphin' class as well, and the German Submarine Consortium is pushing the idea of the Type 212 as the basis for a 'Eurosub' to generate massive savings through commonality of systems and weapons. The only fly in the ointment is the decision of the French to abandon SSK construction.

The saga of the Israeli submarine contract proves what happens when industrial know-how is lost. Israeli's Defence Ministry wanted US military aid to be channelled in the form of submarines, and under the Foreign Military Sales (FMS) and Foreign

Military Funding (FMF) regulations such aid is to be supplied by American contractors. But the US Navy's all-nuclear policy had reduced the choice of submarine builders to Newport News and Electric Boat, neither of which had the necessary expertise. Such capacity could, of course, be re-created, but at prohibitive cost, so the Israeli orders had to be placed with HDW in Germany. The Department of Defense had to make Israel the exception which proves the rule, and the only American-made items in the *Dolphin*, *Dakar* and *Leviathan* are the combat system, the anti-ship missiles and the NT-37F torpedoes. The design is very similar to the Type 212, but without the fuel-cell AIP and with the addition of four external launch tubes for UGM-84C Sub Harpoons.

SCANDINAVIA – 'SUBMARINE 2000'

The same theme of commonality runs through the Royal Swedish Navy's 'Viking' Project. For some years the Navy and builders Kockums have been examining concepts under the heading 'Submarine 2000', but in the last year or two the idea of sharing non-recurring costs with Denmark, Norway and Finland has been promoted by a cost-conscious

Defence Material Command (*Fors Materiel Varets*, [FMV]). The leader of the project would be the Royal Swedish Navy, but the other partners would be able to stipulate departures from the standard criteria, notably in electronics, a field in which national industries would demand a work-share. Although Finland has not operated submarines since World War II, an invitation was extended by the 'Viking' project to the Finnish Navy. The Finns enjoy observer-status but a joint Danish-Norwegian-Swedish naval and technical committee is already working on the details of the project.

THE NETHERLANDS' UNIQUE CONTRIBUTION

The Royal Netherlands Navy has made several unique contributions to submarine design, notably the schnorkel, and this tradition continued after 1945. The 'Dolfijn' class (built 1954–66) adopted a unique triple-hull configuration, with two cylinders as the base. The upper cylinder accommodated the crew, control spaces and weapons, while the two lower cylinders housed the diesel-generators, electric motors and batteries. In 1990, the sole survivor, HNlMS *Zeehond* was bought by RHEUM to serve as

a test-vehicle for the Spectre AIP system. The two 'Zwaardvis' class (1966–72) were based on the Barbel design, while the 2489-tonne (2450-ton) 'Walrus' class (1979–94) were intended to be merely improved variants but ended up as a virtually new design. Increasing the diving depth to 300m (984ft) and adding other advanced features such as X-form rudders made for huge cost-overruns, and it was said that the *Walrus* broke the careers of three admirals before her launch in 1985. Her reputation did not improve when she suffered a disastrous fire 10 months later while fitting out at RDM's yard. The fire distorted the hull and totally destroyed the combat system, but she was rebuilt and re-launched three years later.

The *Walrus* and her sisters have proved to be very capable, and there has been no further bad luck. However, the Royal Netherlands Navy has cut its submarine force to only four boats, and in the process RDM has lost its edge in export markets. At one time it was hoped to sell two 1829-tonne (1800-ton) 'Moray' types to the Navy as a 'pump-primer' for the design, but the refusal of the Netherlands Government to permit the sale of the 'Moray' to Taiwan seems to

have been the yard's last chance. An attempt to win business by selling the 'Zwaardvis' class also failed.

ITALY FORCED TO IMPORT

The Italian Navy started submarine construction once more in the early 1960s, with the four small 'Enrico Toti', but previously nine ex-US Navy boats had been operated.

About 10 years later work started on a new class, based on the ubiquitous 'Barbel' design. The four 'Nazario Sauro' class were followed by two classes incorporating progressive improvements, the two 'Salvatore Pelosi' class and the two 'Primo Longobardo' class (all built in 1986–95). But plans to build a new design, known as S 90 suffered endless financial delays. Finally, the Italian Navy admitted defeat, and announced in 1995 that it had started negotiations with the German Submarine Consortium to buy the Type 212 design. For the foreseeable future the Italian Navy has lost its ability to design and build submarines, although Italian industry is still capable of providing equipment such as combat systems and torpedoes.

Although many analysts have tried to claim that the SSK should be small, ie, displacing not more than 1524 tonnes (1500 tons) on the surface, the current trend is for large SSKs of 2032–3048 tonnes (2000–3000 tons). The reason is the need to provide a capable armament; this in turn forces the designers to incorporate a powerful combat system and a full range of sensors. A comprehensive suite of electronics needs cooling, either by air-conditioning or by chilled water, and the subsystems all demand electrical power. Manpower is expensive, so automation plays its part in keeping running costs under control. For example, the emission of hydrogen from batteries and the heat-level within each cell must be monitored constantly, either by frequent manual inspection or automatically.

ROYAL NAVY CHOOSES SSKS

The Royal Navy's declared ambition of going all-nuclear in the 1970s soon ran into trouble, and in the late 1980s four 'Upholder' class SSKs were built by Vickers Shipbuilding & Engineering Ltd (now known as VSEL and part of GEC Marine). These big boats (2438 tonnes [2400 tons]) had a dual role – training and surveillance in Northern waters – for which they needed range. They also had a powerful armament of 18 torpedoes and missiles. Unfortunately the end of the Cold War robbed them of their surveillance

mission, and the general reduction in funding resulted in these fine boats being decommissioned. They were laid up at VSEL's Barrow-in-Furness shipyard until leased to Canada in March 1998. The French Navy has also been forced to make the hard choice between SSNs and SSKs, and its four 'Agosta' class will be taken out of service by the end of the century.

What has made a major difference to the SSK in recent years has been the emergence of workable AIP systems. The threat from maritime patrol aircraft is now so severe that in a hostile environment (eg, the North Norwegian Sea or the Mediterranean) an SSK cannot afford to use her schnorkel for more than 20 minutes. What is known as the submarine's discretion-rate, the period between battery-chargings, must be extended if the submarine is to regain the advantage. The purpose of AIP systems is to 'float the load' on the batteries, using the AIP system to run the 'hotel services' such as air-conditioning, hot water, auxiliary electrical power, etc, and so keep the batteries fully charged for any emergency.

THE AIP SYSTEM

During World War II the *Kriegsmarine* had experimented with a closed-cycle diesel system as an alternative to the Walter perhydrol-fuelled turbine. Postwar, the Americans and British experimented with high-test peroxide, but the Soviet Navy was more impressed with the *Kreislauf* system, and designed the Project 615 'Quebec' class coastal submarines around the concept. What the Soviets called a 'single propulsion system' ran submerged on an internal supply of liquid oxygen (LOX). The oxygen was added after the exhaust gases were filtered through a lime-based chemical absorbent. The boat could also run its *Kreislauf* diesel in the normal way, using a schnorkel.

The 'Quebec' had three engines, a 32D 900bhp diesel on the centre shaft and two M-50P 700bhp diesels on the outer shafts. In addition a 100hp 'creep' motor was coupled to the centre shaft and a back-up diesel-generator aft. The boat could be run at slow speed using the centreline diesel only. Soviet records suggest that experiments had started before 1941, probably with the small coastal boat *M.92*, and other closed-cycle designs were prepared after the 'Quebec'. Because LOX cannot be stored for any great length of time these 467-tonne (460-ton) boats could not operate far from a base. It was also a dangerous system; at least seven suffered explosions, and one of these, *M.256*, sank after being flooded

Above: HMS *Upholder*, seen here at Portsmouth in August 1991, was one of an intended class of 10 SSKs. The order was cut to four, all of which were leased to the Canadians.

during firefighting efforts. One boat with the Walter turbine AIP system was built, the 965-tonne (950-ton) Project 617 S.99, known to NATO as the 'Whale' type. The *S.99* made 315 dives using her Walter system, in 1956–9, but in May 1959 she was badly damaged by an explosion, and was never repaired. After these boats were decommissioned in the early 1960s interest in AIP lapsed, but recently the Russian Rubin Bureau announced that it can offer an AIP system for the new 'Amur' type SSK. Information released shows that it is a fuel-cell system (see below).

The most successful AIP system so far is the Stirling engine. Developed from a patent dating back to 1816, the Stirling cycle burns diesel fuel in pure oxygen, in a pressure vessel. The Swedish submarine builders Kockums AB of Malmö own the rights to the Stirling engine, and tested its V4-275R 75kW engine in the serving submarine *Nacken*. This proved successful, with less vibration than a conventional diesel-generator, and considerably lower noise levels. In fact it is possible to conduct a conversation while

standing alongside a running Stirling engine. Since then the A 19 type 'Gotland' class have been built from the outset with Stirling engines, and the system has been evaluated by a number of navies. Despite rumours of submarines running entirely on four Stirling engines, Kockums denies this, pointing out that the amount of LOX required would be impossible to fit into the submarine's hull.

The German Navy followed a different route, funding Siemens and HDW in the development of a Proton Exchange Membrane (PEM) fuel cell capable of generating 40kW. As with the Stirling principle, the idea is an old one, dating back to 1839. In essence a fuel-cell reverses the process of electrolysis, using a chemical reaction to combine hydrogen and oxygen, thereby producing electrical energy, heat and water. The heart of the PEM system is a solid polymer electrolyte in the form of an ion exchange membrane in contract with a platinum catalyst and carbon paper electrodes. The membrane is positioned between the fluid flow field and the cooling units in such a manner that hydrogen ions pass through it and combine with hydrogen anions. As long as hydrogen and oxygen are supplied the fuel cell will continue to produce power.

A single fuel cell cannot produce more than 1.48V and therefore several must be stacked to form a

Left: HMS *Ursula*, the third of the 'Upholder' class. In Canadian service she will be armed with the US Navy's Mk 48 Model 4 torpedo and a Canadian towed sonar array.

system is its use of the same diesel for schnorkelling or as an AIP unit, a great saving in cost. The system is being marketed by TNSW and RDM (as the Spectre system). The TNSW trials with *U.1* had the rare benefit of comparing like with like: both the fuel cell and the CCD being tested in the same hull.

The only other AIP system available is the French (*Module d'Energie Sous-Marin Autonome* [MESMA]) system, which uses an oxygen-ethanol fuelled steam turbine. Conceived in the early 1980s by the Bertin company, it was taken up by DCN, the French Navy's design and procurement bureau, in collaboration with *Empresa Nacional Bazan* in Spain. Although the French Navy has not installed MESMA in a submarine, it has been sold to Pakistan for fitting to new Agosta-90B type SSKs.

The excitement over AIP has led to exaggerated claims about its potential. Some commentators claim that the advent of AIP has created a third category of submarine, the SSK+AIP, but the fact remains that only one navy has a modern AIP system operating. Three more will have systems in service after the turn of the century (counting Italy's acquisition of the Type 212 design), but a number of experienced operators are still not sufficiently convinced to commit themselves.

FUTURE DEVELOPMENTS

AIP enthusiasts point to potential developments. The CCD system has great promise, with such improvements as electronic fuel-injection and electronically actuated valves. These improvements will allow the operator to select engine-characteristics from a menu of choices. The Solid Oxide Fuel Cell (SOFC) would use natural gas as fuel, resulting in a single propulsion system for surface and submerged propulsion. Siemens is also known to be working on a fuel cell using methanol as the base fuel to generate hydrogen.

In theory none of the weapons and sensors which equip SSNs are unsuitable for SSKs, but size is critical. A large internal volume is required to accommodate modern electronics and the fuel and batteries needed for reasonable endurance. As U-boats found in World War I, the number of weapon reloads is also critical in deciding how long a submarine can remain effective. As the number of sensors has increased, so has the demand for processing power and displays.

module. The main drawback to the system is the cost of materials, and HDW has so far not offered it for export. The Federal German Navy tested a 100kW prototype installation in the old Type 205 boat *U.1*, and the Type 212 boats currently under construction will have a 400kW version.

OTHER AIP SYSTEMS

After the fuel cell trials the *U.1* was made available by the Navy to TNSW for trials of a closed-cycle diesel AIP system (CCD). This has the advantage of being simple, the most complex part being the water-absorption system developed by Cosworth Engineering. The engine exhaust gas is 'scrubbed' with water to remove the carbon dioxide, and in the same process the water vapour is condensed. Surplus carbon dioxide is eliminated by adding a small quantity of argon gas. The great virtue of the CCD

Above: Four 'Sauro' class boats were ordered for the Italian Navy in 1972, based on the US Navy's 'Barbel' class. Since then four improved variants have been built.

Even automation is not the whole answer, because a minimum number of people are needed to cope with battle damage and system failures. Over-reliance on automation results in crew-fatigue on long patrols. During and after the Falklands War the Royal Navy's 'Oberons' were spending 42 days in transit and on patrol, 14,816km (more than 8000 miles) from a dockyard. The strain on the crew after such a long patrol has to be seen at first hand. Even after the Argentine surrender and the formal end of military activity some 'Oberons' had to avoid Argentine SSKs, not knowing what their opponent's rules of engagement might be. This meant that the British submarine had to behave as if her opponent was hostile, but without the ability to take any offensive action to remove the threat.

The prestige of submarines and their undoubted deterrent value means that more navies will acquire them in the next decade. But the enormous through-life cost of SSNs and their unsuitablity for inshore operations means that the SSK will remain a much more attractive option for the lesser navies. US Naval Intelligence predicts that many more SSKs will be in the hands of non-aligned or unstable countries. Iran's acquisition of three 'Kilos' since 1988 caused something close to panic in Washington, although the Iranians seem to be interested only in safeguarding their coastal waters from hostile incursions. It is a chilling thought that if Saddam Hussein had possessed submarines in 1991, the Coalition naval forces could not have operated with so much freedom in the Northern Gulf.

CHAPTER SIX

Modern Nuclear Submarines

The nuclear submarine, with its high speed and an endurance limited only by the need to feed its crew, has emerged as a modern capital ship. Progress in nuclear technology has been evolutionary rather than revolutionary, but the range of weapons now includes subsurface-to-surface missiles and land-attack cruise missiles.

By the early 1960s many US Navy submariners were beginning to express their unease at the trend to lower underwater speeds, from the 28 knots of the 'Thresher' (SS-593) class to the 25 knots of the 'Sturgeon' (SSN-637) class and the 'Narwhal' (SSN-671), down to the 23-knot 'Glenard P Lipscomb' (SSN-685). Meanwhile, in the Soviet Union, the Navy's SSNs were making their own contribution to the sense of unease.

Left: HMS *Vanguard*, the first of a new class of Royal Navy SSBNs armed with the D5 Trident ballistic missile system, was rolled out in March 1992 by her builders, VSEL.

An American SSN would be able to detect a noisy Soviet SSN at long range, but in all probability she would have to move fast to reach a firing position. It was believed that a 5-knot margin was the minimum for an SSN operating in a sprint-and-drift mode while patrolling a chokepoint barrier such as the Greenland-Iceland-UK (GIUK) Gap. Sprint-and-drift tactics are so-called because the SSN must slow down or 'drift' to use her sonars to maximum advantage and then 'sprint' to a predicted interception point. The barrier submarine might lose sonar contact, and only speed would suffice to regain the initiative, and even if the enemy SSN detected her

Above: The French submarine *l'Inflexible* was the first of a new generation of strategic submarines, a stage between the 'Redoutable' class and the 'Triomphant' class.

Right: The French *Triomphant* is the first of a planned total of four SNLEs. She and the *Temeraire* are armed with the M4 missile system, which will be replaced by the M5.

first, high underwater speed would enable her to reach a firing position first.

High speed was also seen as a valuable asset for attacks on hostile submarines detected by long-range acoustic detection systems. In most areas maritime patrol aircraft would be able to attack any targets found, but in areas where the Soviets might have air superiority, SSNs would be the only safe way to attack enemy submarines. Equally, a burst of high speed would enable a submarine on surveillance duty to evade pursuers.

Even more important in the debate was the value of the SSN as an escort for aircraft carriers. The knowledge that the Soviet Navy intended to use its new SSGNs and SSNs to counter the threat from US carrier bombers fuelled the debate. It was known that Soviet submarine tactics envisaged attacks from off the carrier's bow. The attacker would not need to be as fast as the carrier; she would expect to have been cued into position by the Soviet ocean surveillance system (OSS). Hitherto fast carriers had been considered to be virtually immune to submarine attack because SSKs could only attack from very limited arcs ahead of their

targets. It had been assumed that submarines lying in wait ahead of the carrier would be easy to evade, but the SSN was an altogether tougher proposition.

An escorting SSN challenged that assumption. She could use her long-range sonar to sweep ahead of the carrier, drifting from time to time and then sprinting to catch up. But to this a minimum speed of 30 knots was seen as essential. Despite widespread public claims not contradicted by the submariners, very few nuclear submarines were capable of such speeds (even the fast 'Skipjacks' had only just achieved 30 knots). This was not a new idea; the Royal Navy had previously experimented with HMS *Dreadnought* in this role, and the results were made available to the US Navy, which had done similar pioneer work with Task Group 'Alfa' earlier.

US NAVY SSNS –A RETHINK

Against this background Admiral Rickover proposed a redesign of the D1G/D2G surface-ship reactor with double the horsepower of the S5W plant. He envisaged a combination of the new reactor (later

designated S6G) with the bow sonar and weapon system of the 'Sturgeon', and the simplified hull structure of the 'Narwhal'. Some effort was put into reducing the area of the sail, because it was a major source of drag, but the price was heavy. Whereas the 'Sturgeon' class could turn their sail-mounted diving plans to the vertical to 'chop' their way through thin ice, the new sail of the new SSN was too low for the planes to be moved through 90 degrees. She would also be much bigger and so much more expensive, yet she would have the same number of weapon launch tubes (four Mk 63 type, abaft the big bow sonar and angled out). On the positive side, the bigger internal volume allowed the weapon-load to be increased from 23 to 26 Mk 48 heavyweight torpedoes.

Like all high-technology projects, both civil and military, the new SSN took years of project-definition and coordination of all the elements of design. Detailed design did not start until early 1969, with great attention paid to simplicity to reduce costs, but with no reduction in silencing. Torpedo-tube design was improved to allow torpedoes to be fired at

maximum speed. Previous submarines had found it impossible to open the bow doors at high speed, so a new type of rotating door was adopted. The first-of-class, the USS *Los Angeles* (SSN-688) was not laid down until January 1972, and she joined the fleet nearly five years later. Nineteen years later the 62nd boat, the commissioning of the USS *Cheyenne* (SSN-773) brought to a close the biggest group of SSNs ever built to a single design.

The reason for such a long production run was uncertainty about successors, and by 1995 the design

Above: The streamlined fin of the USS *Oklahoma City*. The 'Los Angeles' design emphasised high pursuit speed by doubling the output of the S6G reactor.

was beginning to look dated. It is misleading, however, to imply that the design remained static throughout the two decades. The intention had been to equip the new class with a digital combat system to improve reliability and save weight. This was not ready in time, and the first 12 boats were given the Mk 113 analog system. The first with the Mk 117 was the Dallas (SSN-700), but the earlier boats and the 'Sturgeon' class were eventually given the system. Under the Fiscal Year 1983 (FY '83) programme the Mk 117 system was modified to handle the UUM-44A-2 Subroc nuclear anti-submarine missile, and in 1978 the UGM-84A Sub Harpoon anti-ship missile was introduced. The principal sensor is the AN/BQQ-5 digital set, using a spherical bow array and the AN/BQR-21 conformal array with digital multi-beam steering (DIMUS). Later the BQR-15 passive towed array was added; it was normally stowed in a channel on the starboard side of the casing, and streamed through a tube on the starboard diving plane.

To give these submarines a massive increase in long-range firepower, not only against ship targets but against land targets as well, they were given the BGM-109 Tomahawk cruise missile. This changed

Left: USS *Von Steuben* was one of the first generation of Polaris A3 armed strategic submarines. She was laid up in 1993 after 30 years of continuous deterrent patrols.

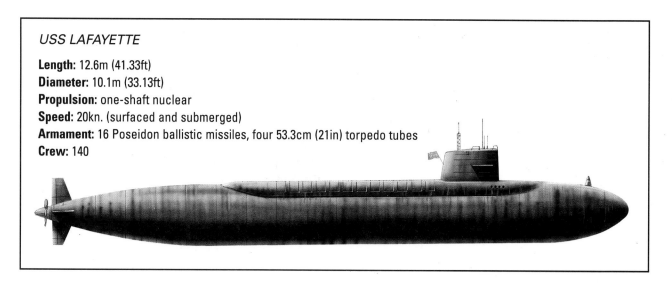

USS LAFAYETTE

Length: 12.6m (41.33ft)
Diameter: 10.1m (33.13ft)
Propulsion: one-shaft nuclear
Speed: 20kn. (surfaced and submerged)
Armament: 16 Poseidon ballistic missiles, four 53.3cm (21in) torpedo tubes
Crew: 140

the weapon load, which now comprised 14 Mk 48 torpedoes, four Sub Harpoons and eight Tomahawks, all tube-launched. The first of the class with this capability was the *La Jolla* (SSN-701) in 1981, but the first to become operational was the *Atlanta* (SSN-712), towards the end of 1983. The next step was to provide 12 vertical-launch tubes in the void space between the bow sonar and the forward dome bulkhead. The first of this group was the USS *Providence* (SSN-719).

Cost was rising, from $221 million for the *Los Angeles* in 1976 to $495 million 10 years later. By the early 1980s under-ice operations were assuming more importance, and a measure of redesign was necessary. This took the form of strengthening the sail and moving the forward diving planes from the sail to the bow, and making them retractable. They were also given the new BSY-1 integrated combat system, and the package of improvements resulted in the new designation SSN-688I ('Improved'). The first of this series was the *San Juan* (SSN-751), which was commissioned in 1988.

If evidence was needed that the 'Los Angeles' class was in production for too long, figures published in 1996 showed that four of the class had been decommissioned and were waiting for a decision on recycling of their reactor cores: the former *Baton Rouge* (SSN-689), damaged beyond repair in an underwater collision with a Soviet SSN, *Omaha* (SSN-692), *Cincinnati* (SSN-693) and *New York City* (SSN-696). By 1997 two more had been decommissioned and 11 more will be gone by 2000. The *Memphis* (SSN-691) was taken out of service in 1989 to carry out trials of advanced underwater systems

Above: A total of 31 'Lafayette' class SSBNs were built in 1961-67 and all received the new Poseidon missile, successor to the A3 Polaris missile.

The US Navy's 41 SSBNs were also beginning to show their age, both in terms of their hull lives and in the effectiveness of their C3 Poseidon SLBM systems. The knowledge that the R-39 Rif-M (SS-N-20 'Sturgeon') SLBM could hit cities in the United States from the 'bastion' in the Barents Sea concentrated minds in the Pentagon. Taifun is a three-stage solid-fuelled missile with six to ten 100-kiloton MIRV warheads. Its range is more than 8000km (4319.6 miles) and the circular error of probability is no more than 1.9km (1.02 miles). To match this awesome threat the US Navy funded the development of a Poseidon replacement, the C4 Trident I. When the baseline design was completed in 1971 the US Government was negotiating the first Strategic Arms Limitation Treaty (SALT I), and President Nixon was anxious to find a strategic system which could enter service within the five-year term of the treaty.

THE C4 TRIDENT

The C4 Trident (initially designated the Underwater Launched Missile System or ULMS) was intended to double the range of Poseidon without exceeding its 'ownership cost'. Advanced development began at the end of December 1971 and the prototype C4X1 flew in January 1977. It was also designed to replace C3 Poseidon in some of the later 'Lafayette' class SSBNs. The launch tubes in the new SSBNs would be designed to be replaceable by tubes large enough to accommodate the larger D5 Trident II, planned to enter service in 1990.

The statistics of Trident are awesome. Compared to the Poseidon, the C4 Trident I (UGM-96A) has a range of 8056.2km (4350 miles), but with a CEP of 475.2m (1500ft) it had similar accuracy. It has about the same 'throw-weight', launching eight Mk 4 re-entry vehicles with W76 100-kiloton warheads. Increased range is achieved by extending its effective length with an 'aerospike' during launch. This reduces drag by half and adds about 556km (300 miles). Improved propellant allows the missile to burn its fuel in the first and second stages, and calculate appropriate trajectory for the third.

The D5 Trident II (UGM-133A) uses the same Mk 98 fire control system (Mod 1 in US Navy SSBNs, Mod 2 in the British 'Vanguard' class) but adds a gravity sensor and a new navigation sonar. The newer Mk 6 guidance system, developed from the Mk 5 in Trident I, uses global positioning (GPS) to reduce the CEP to 118.8m (389.7ft), equivalent to land-based ICBMs for the first time. The number of warheads is variable, with eight W87 warheads being used for early tests, and some tests done with 10 smaller warheads. However, for arms limitation the missile is agreed to have no more than eight independent warheads, carried by the Mk 5 'delivery bus'. The British Trident IIs will carry no more than three

Below: HMS *Vanguard* on sea trials in 1992. A single hit from one of the three warheads on her D5 Trident missiles will destroy 60 per cent of a major city.

AT-3K Chevaline warheads, as in the earlier A3 Polaris system. The missile first flew from a submarine in August 1989, but several failures caused its entry into service to be delayed until March 1990.

THE NEW US SSBNS

The new SSBNs, known as the 'Ohio' (SSBN-726) class, were impressive, 16,256.8-tonne (16,000-ton) submarines armed with 24 SLBMs. They were the biggest submarines yet built for the US Navy, although dwarfed by the Soviet 'Typhoon' class. A single S8G reactor rated at 35,000hp drives them at 25 knots. Although acquisition cost was high, this was offset by longer periods between overhauls. They operate 70-day patrols, with 25-day overhaul periods in between each. They are designed to have a one-year overhaul every nine years, giving a 66 per cent availability, as compared with 55 per cent for the older SSBNs. Initial plans were for 20 boats, and that was increased to 24, but under the Strategic Arms

Reduction Talks the US Government agreed to cut the total back to 18. The class was plagued by delays; work was not started on the *Ohio* until April 1976, but she did not start trials until June 1981 (the scheduled date was December 1977). After lengthy delays the order was finally placed at the end of 1997 to fit new launch-tubes to four of the older 'Ohio' class to enable them to fire Trident II. Starting in 1998 Northrop Grumman will build 24 launch systems for the USS *Alaska* (SSBN-732), with the *Nevada* (SSBN-733), *Henry M Jackson* (SSBN-730) and *Alabama* (SSBN-731) to follow. The four oldest SSBNs will not be modified, and the SSBN force will eventually shrink to 14 boats by 2002, the year before the START II agreement takes effect.

THE NEW SOVIET SSNS

The new Soviet SSNs which had caused all this activity were the Project 670 *Skat* ('Charlie I') and Project 671 *Ersh* ('Victor') types, which first appeared in the mid-1960s. But even the Project 627A *Kit* ('November') was giving serious cause for worry. In February 1968 a 'November' intercepted the nuclear-

Left: An operator carries out a simulated firing of a Trident missile aboard an 'Ohio' class submarine. Very few rounds are fired because of the cost – and even fewer live rounds!

Below: The 'Ohio' class SSBNs were designed to spend longer periods between overhauls and to remain on patrol for 70 days. This means a major saving in cost terms.

USS *OHIO*

Length: 170.7m (560ft)
Diameter: 12.8m (50ft)
Propulsion: one-shaft nuclear
Speed: 25kn. (surfaced and submerged)
Armament: 24 ballistic missiles, four 53.3cm (21in) torpedo tubes
Crew: 133

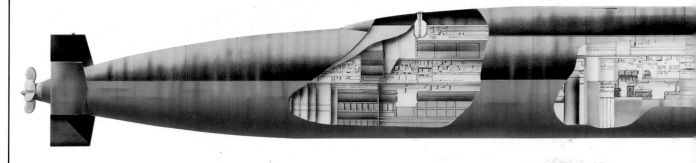

Above: USS *Florida* running on the surface during her sea trials. She and other units of the 'Ohio' class will be decommissioned to comply with disarmament treaties.

powered carrier USS *Enterprise* (CVN-65) en route for Vietnam. Although she was slower, the Soviet SSN used data from the ocean surveillance system to achieve a theoretically perfect interception. The higher performance of the 'Charlie' and Victor' designs made them even more of a threat, and to make matters worse, some overheated analysis of Soviet industrial capacity led to an estimate of 20 new SSNs

a year. Through judicious leaks on both sides of the Atlantic this very pessimistic figure rapidly became 'fact', causing something close to paranoia in military and political circles.

Recently published figures from Russian sources show that Russian SSN building was more modest:

18 'Victor Is' between 1967 and 1974
11 'Charlie Is' between 1967 and 1974
7 'Victor IIs' between 1972 and 1978
6 'Charlie IIs' between 1975 and 1980
26 'Victor IIIs' between 1978 and 1987

Above: The Russian Project 670A 'Charlie I' type SSGN introduced the P-20L SS-N-7 long-range anti-ship missile intended to attack US Navy aircraft carriers.

A total of 68 in 20 years amounts to only three-to-four SSNs per annum, comparable to the 'Los Angeles' class. But against this must be set the greatly enhanced performance of the Project 671RTM *Shchuka* ('Victor III'). On a surfaced displacement of 5029 tonnes (4950 tons), it had a twin VM-42 reactor plant driving a single-shaft OK-300 turbine; its 31,000hp output produced an underwater speed of 30 knots. In addition there were two auxiliary propellers driven by electric 'creep' motors. Early units had a single seven-bladed propeller, but most had an unusual arrangement of tandem four-bladed propellers. The electronics included a Skat-KS bow sonar, an MT-70 set for under-ice navigation, an MRK-50 navigation radar, Bulava electronic support measures (ESM), and a wake sensor. The armament was four 53.3cm (21in) torpedo tubes and two 65cm (25.6in) launch tubes for P-100 (SS-N-22) missiles.

The 'Victor III' demonstrated clearly that the West could no longer rely on the noisiness of Soviet submarines. Raft-mounted machinery and careful attention to other noise-reduction measures showed that the information on the crucial role played by the US and NATO's Sound Underwater Surveillance (SOSUS) long-range passive arrays handed over by the Walkers had been put to good use. These spies had made available the 'burn-bags' of SOSUS intercepts, showing how accurately Soviet submarines were being tracked.

Espionage may have played another part in the 'Victor III' development. Most if not all 26 were later given the 'Viking' combat system, believed to be based on the Norwegian MSI-90U system. The chain was a complex one, starting with American ire against the Japanese firm Toshiba for supplying very precise milling machines to produce non-cavitating propeller blades, but in fact the technology came to Japan via the Norwegian firm Kongsberg (later NFT) which made the MSI-90U combat system for German and Norwegian submarines. If such a technology 'pinch' occurred, it would have given the Soviets crucial parameters of NATO's anti-submarine tactics (both German and Norwegian submarines played leading roles in NATO's efforts to contain the Soviet Navy).

INFLUENTIAL RUSSIAN DESIGN

The other Soviet design which exercised a major influence over US Navy thinking on submarines was the Project 705 Lira, the notorious 'Alfa' class mentioned in an earlier chapter. Work on this project started in late 1958 or early 1959 at the Specialist

Design Bureau No.143 (SKB-143 in Leningrad (renamed the Malakhit Bureau in the 1970s). The starting point seems to have been a small but fast submarine intended to hunt other submarines, similar in concept to a proposal by Admiral Rickover for an SSKN. The speed proposed was 40 knots, twice that of the *Nautilus*, on a surface displacement of only 1524 tonnes (1500 tons).

The new submarine was to have a single titanium hull, with a single reactor and turbine plant driving a single shaft, and fully automated controls. This would cut the crew to only nine officers and three senior petty officers. However, it was soon clear to the designer, A B Petrov, that the desired speed and an acceptable level of reliability could not be achieved on 1524 tonnes (1500 tons). An increase to 2337 tonnes (2300 tons) was recommended, but the SKB-143 team tried to avoid this by abandoning full shielding of the reactor compartment, using instead light-weight 'shade' protection between the reactor and the accommodation spaces forward. This was understandably unpopular because of the danger from the accumulation of highly radioactive Polonium-210 in the irradiated lead-bismuth coolant.

Not even these desperate measures could get the displacement down to 1930 tonnes (1900 tons), and the Soviet Navy would not accept the idea of a single-hull boat operating at great distances from its base support. After the preliminary design was presented at the end of 1960 a new Council of Ministers decree was issued the following May, insisting on double-hull titanium construction and a larger crew of at least 18 (raised to 27). The new sketch design was ready by the end of the same year, when the technical design requirement (TTZ) was issued.

The first of four Project 705 boats was laid down at the Admiralty Yard in Leningrad in June 1968, long-lead items having been ordered four years earlier. A production version, Project 705K, was paradoxically laid down at the Northern Machine Construction yard in Severodvinsk slightly earlier, in November 1967. The completion date of the prototype *K.377* has for some reason not been published (it was in the early 1970s), but *K.123*, the first Project 705K, was not completed until the end of 1977.

The new submarine was armed with six 53.3cm (21in) launch tubes and 18 torpedoes and RPK-2

Below: The Russian Project 941 'Typhoon' class are the largest submarines ever built. They were intended as last-resort weapons, lying on the seabed for up to a year.

Above: The Royal Navy's 'Astute' class SSNs were formerly designated the Batch 2 'Trafalgar' class, but they will have a more powerful PWR 2 reactor plant.

Right: HMS *Resolution* was the first of four SSBNs armed with the A3 Polaris missile. The Polaris SSBN project was unusual in being completed on time and within budget.

Viyuga (SS-N-15) anti-submarine missiles, using a UBZ rapid-loading system. The electronics included a Kerch low-frequency/high-frequency bow sonar, with a 1.45-m (4.75ft) high cylindrical array, a high-frequency Zhgut ('Mouse Roar') mine-avoidance sonar, and an Akkord fire control system. The Project 705 boats had two OK-550 reactors, with three steam generators driving two steam turbines. This 38,000hp plant produced the staggering speed of 43 knots underwater, approaching the still unbroken record of the Project 661 'Papa'. But the rumours of a diving depth of 900m (2952.7ft) put about in the West were nowhere near the truth. The 'Alfa' had a designed operating depth of 320–350m (1049–1148ft) and a crush-depth of 400m (1312ft).

Major changes were made during construction at the Navy's insistence. The three watertight compartments were increased to seven, leading to a very unusual configuration to get around equipment already installed. Thus the bulkhead between the first and second compartments formed part of the first compartment's deck in some places. Those of the third compartment were concave.

The three Project 705K boats were driven by the more advanced BM-40A reactor plant, using only two steam generators operating at much higher pressure.

The original 705 prototype suffered a serious reactor accident only a year after being commissioned, and because the liquid metal coolant was allowed to cool down nothing could be done to repair it. After the loss of the experimental *Komsomolets* in 1989 the Naval Staff decided to withdraw all the Project 705 and 705K boats as potentially unsafe. According to

Russian sources the design had lost its charm by 1973, not just because of its huge cost, but because it was so difficult to maintain. Marshal Ustinov, the Defence Minister, visited the laid-up *K.377* and commented that she was too cramped and impossible to repair. But, whatever criticisms can be levelled at the 'Alfa', the Russian designers had shown the world that they could challenge orthodox thinking. Things in the submarine business would never be the same again.

ANOTHER RUSSIAN SUCCESS – THE 'AKULA'

Mention has been made in a previous chapter of the advances in the 'Mike' and 'Sierra' type SSNs, but the Soviet Navy had another card up its sleeve. This was the

Project 971 *Bars*, known to the West as the 'Akula' (confusingly, NATO's names now included a traditional Russian submarine name). Although configured like a classic SSN, this design began life in 1972 as an SSGN armed with contemporary anti-ship missiles, but in 1978–80 it was reworked to become a platform for the S-10 *Granat* (SS-N-21 'Sampson') 'Tomahawkski' strategic cruise missile. For that reason it was built with two 53.3cm (21in) torpedo tubes and four 65cm (25.6in) launch tubes for the missiles, although later units have six additional bow tubes outside the pressure hull, providing more firepower. The corresponding SSN type was to be the 'Sierra' but the steel-hulled 'Akula' was so much cheaper that it was turned into a general-purpose attack submarine, although two knots slower.

The sonar suite corresponds to that of the latest 'Victor IIIs', (MGK-503 Skat) but with an additional flank array extending for about a third of the hull. The power plant is, however, new, with double-silencing, rafted machinery and the raft itself isolated from the hull. This makes the 'Akula' the quietest of all Soviet submarines. The OK-650B reactor is the same as the 'Oscar', 'Sierra' and 'Typhoon' designs, driving a single turbine and developing 43,000hp, equal to an underwater speed of 35 knots. The single shaft drives a seven-bladed propeller. Diving depth is 450m (1476ft), according to Russian sources, with a crush-depth of 550m (1804ft).

Seven 'Bars' class were built at Komsomolsk in 1982–95, but an eighth, to be named *Nerpa*, was apparently not completed. The yard closed in 1993, possibly with two more of this class on order or laid down. Another five were built at Severodvinsk by 1994, but two more were apparently unfinished. As

Above: A dramatic photograph of the 'Los Angeles' class submarine USS *Birmingham* conducting emergency surfacing trials in the Pacific Ocean.

with other Soviet and Russian designs, there has been a well-orchestrated 'Akula Panic' in the West. Their reputation rests not only on their quietness but also on their formidable armament. The RK-55 Shkval rocket-propelled torpedo is reputed to be a deadly weapon, and the 65cm (25.6in) long-range super-heavyweight will cripple even a 101,605-tonne (100,000-ton) aircraft carrier.

RUSSIA REASSERTS HERSELF

In spite of its dire economic problems the Russian Government is trying desperately to regain some of the trappings of a superpower. It is significant that SSBNs of the Northern Fleet still go to sea on a regular basis, and a new series of designs is appearing. Such activity is essential if the industrial base is not wither away, and also to replace obsolete tonnage. The Project 667

'Murena', 'Kalmar' and 'Delfin' class ('Delta I, III and IV') SSBNs entered service between 1972 and 1992, and the Project 941 'Akula' class ('Typhoon') between 1981 and 1989. Two of the 'Typhoon' type have been laid up, and it is inevitable that some of the 'Deltas' will follow soon. To replace them the first Project 955 'Bory' type was started in 1996, with a view to the prototype *Yuri Dolgorukiy* being delivered in 2002. According to the US Navy's estimates, she will be armed with 12 R-39UTTKh (SS-N-28 'Grom') or R-29RM (SS-N-23 'Skiff') SLBMs. The 'Skiff' is the first Russian MIRV submarine missile, and already arms the 'Delta IVs'. Under arms limitation rules it has four

Left: HMS *Conqueror* returning to Faslane Submarine Base. In 1982 she torpedoed the Argentinian cruiser *General Belgrano* during the Falklands War.

100-kiloton warheads, a range of 8300km (4481.6 miles) and a CEP of 500–900m (1640.4–2952.7ft). The 'Grom' is an improved R-39 Rif-M (SS-N-20 'Sturgeon') with eight MIRV warheads, and the same range and CEP as the 'Skiff'. Its nomination for the 'Bory' class is said to depend on whether it will be ready in time; if not, the proven R-29RM will be chosen.

THE 'SEVERODVINSK'

The corresponding combined SSN/SSGN design is the Project 885 'Severodvinsk' class, of which the prototype was laid down in December 1993 at the Severodvinsk shipyard. According to the US Navy she displaces 9652 tonnes (9500 tons) on the surface and is driven by a single reactor and twin GT3A turbines for a submerged speed of 28 knots. Armament includes four 65cm (25.6in) launch tubes forward, and two 53.3cm (21in) tubes, with a mixture of 30 weapons, including RPK-2 *Viyuga* (SS-N-15) anti-submarine missiles. This is an equivalent of the defunct American Subroc, also with a nuclear warhead to compensate for the inaccuracy of contemporary long-range sonars. The main offensive armament is a silo of eight vertical-launch anti-ship or land-attack missiles. According to the US Navy this will be the SS-N-26 'Sapless', but the exact nature of the weapon is still unclear. Elsewhere, SS-N-26 is described as the P-800 Yakhont, a formidable ramjet-powered supersonic missile (Mach 2-2.5), but the P-1000 Vulkan may be the submarine-launched version. A similar system called Oniks is said to have been installed for trials in the Project 670M 'Charlie II' B.452 some years ago. Although the building schedule seems very optimistic, bearing in mind the chaotic state of the naval shipyards, the 'Severodvinsk' promises to be a formidable antagonist.

BRITISH DEVELOPMENTS

The Royal Navy had been content to follow a different line to the US Navy in its SSN design philosophy, being content to trade off maximum speed against quietness. In 1977 the first of seven 'Trafalgar' class was ordered – 4775-tonne (4700-ton) boats driven by a single PWR 1 reactor and twin turbines at a maximum underwater speed of about 28 knots. The first-of-class was commissioned in 1983, and the last, HMS *Triumph*, in 1991. The basic hull of the earlier 'Swiftsure' was retained, but with much greater attention to silencing; the second

Below: HMS *Talent* is one of the Royal Navy's 'Trafalgar' class SSNs. They are among the quietest submarines in service thanks to a well-thought out design.

Above: HMS *Triumph* is the last of seven 'Trafalgar' class SSNs built for the Royal Navy in 1979–91. She and her sisters are to be rearmed with Tomahawk cruise missiles.

boat, HMS *Turbulent*, was given a shrouded pumpjet propulsor in place of the standard seven-bladed skewback propeller, and this was continued for the remaining five boats. After completion all had their hulls coated with anechoic tiling.

Design studies for a follow-on started in 1987, designated the SSN-20 because the first boat would be the 20th in the series which started with HMS *Dreadnought*. Influenced by the fevered debate on Soviet capabilities in the United States the British submariners overplayed their hand, asking for a new

reactor plant to improve on the as-yet undelivered PWR 2, a new combat system to succeed the as-yet undelivered SMCS, and a new torpedo to succeed the as-yet undelivered Spearfish. Project definition started late in 1989, but it was clear to all but the submarine community that these demands were unrealistic. In 1991 the Treasury, looking for excuses to make major cuts, told the Navy that the proposed design did not incorporate 'sufficient advanced technology' to justify the £400 million per hull (excluding research and development).

In November 1991, VSEL was awarded a contract for a year-long design study for the Batch 2 'Trafalgar' Class (B2TC), and despite this transparent fiction, a radically new design, the 'Astute' class, was ordered in 1997 to replace the three oldest 'Swiftsures' early in the

next century. The major external change will be in the hull form, and internally they will have a variant of the successful SMCS command system, the PWR 2 reactor plant developing nearly twice the power of the PWR 1 (27,000hp), the new 2076 integrated sonar system, Spearfish Mod 1 heavyweight torpedoes, Sub Harpoon anti-ship missiles and Tomahawk cruise missiles. The 'Astute' class will displace 6401 tonnes (6300 tons) on the surface (6909 tonnes [6800 tons] submerged), and weapon stowage will increase to 38 rounds.

All seven 'Trafalgars' and possibly three 'Swiftsures' will receive a major upgrade, with the 2076 sonar. Some have already received the SMCS command system, and in 1998 HMS *Splendid* goes to sea with the first operational Block III version of the Tomahawk cruise missile in the Royal Navy. This conversion is comparatively simple, involving a small interface unit to allow the SMCS command system to send instructions to the Tomahawk Weapon Control System (TWCS). The Royal Navy has bought 65 Tomahawks at a cost of $288 million; the integration is done by Lockheed Martin under a separate contract.

The SMCS command system is claimed to have more than 20 times the processing power of previous systems, but at lower acquisition and through-life costs. Development began at the end of 1986, and the first was installed in a shore development facility in mid-1990. This system then went to sea in the SSBN HMS *Vanguard* in 1992, and the first two SSNs to receive it were HMS *Swiftsure* and HMS *Trafalgar* in 1995.

POST COLD-WAR POLICIES

The Royal Navy also needed to replace its four 'Resolution' class SSBNs, which were suffering from problems with their reactors after 20 years in continuous service. Following an acrimonious debate between unilateral nuclear disarmers and critics of the British deterrent policy purely on grounds of cost, the decision was made in 1980 to buy the D5 Trident II system for four new SSBNs. Trident I was deemed to be adequate for the Royal Navy's needs, but as it was coming out of production there was no choice but to go for Trident II. As VSEL was now the only submarine-building shipyard in the United Kingdom all four of the 'Vanguard' class were ordered from the Barrow-in-Furness yard. HMS *Vanguard* was built in 1986–93, followed by HMS *Victorious* and HMS *Vigilant*, while the last, HMS *Vengeance*, is to be delivered in 1999.

These 14,224.7-tonne (14,000-ton) submarines are driven by the new PWR 2 reactor plant developing 27,000hp through two turbines. Underwater speed is 25 knots. To keep costs down the Trident missiles are leased from the US Navy, an arrangement which allows missiles to be maintained and supported from the King's Bay SSBN base in Georgia. These submarines have a Type 2054 integrated sonar suite, which includes the 2043 active/passive bow array, a 2044 reelable towed array and a 2045 intercept sonar. With the end of the Cold War critics have tried to claim that these SSBNs have no role, and to counter such arguments the Navy has initiated studies into a tactical (ie, conventional) modification to Trident or a sub-strategic role, with a single low-yield nuclear warhead. Another option looked at was a partial conversion of some launch tubes to fire cruise

Below: The second-generation Royal Navy SSNs have proved very successful. They are scheduled to receive the new 2076 integrated sonar system and Tomahawk missiles.

HMS *SWIFTSURE*

Length: 82.9m (271.98ft)
Diameter: 9.8m (32.15ft)
Propulsion: one-shaft nuclear
Speed: 20kn./30kn. (surfaced/submerged)
Armament: five 53.3cm (21in) torpedo tubes, Sub Harpoon missiles
Crew: 116

missiles. Apart from the waste of money involved in scrapping new SSBNs, the British Government defends the decision to retain a nuclear deterrent, pointing out that the proliferation of nuclear weapons makes deterrence even more relevant. As a political supporter said, 'Trident will not stop the Soviet Union from invading the British Isles, but it would mean a bad Monday morning in more than one Russian city'.

When Ronald Reagan became president in 1981 he was determined to reverse what most military people regarded as the decline in America's ability to defend its interest against the Soviet Union. His Secretary of the Navy, John Lehman, was determined to rebuild the fleet, and his submariners advised him that the best policy was to go on the offensive in time of war. This meant penetrating the 'bastions' to get at the Soviet submarines, rather than waiting behind barriers until the Soviets chose their moment to attack.

THE US NAVY – A FRESH START

The change of policy also accounted for that doughty old warrior Admiral Rickover, who was retired by Lehman with the backing of the President. Rickover

Above: HMS *Vanguard* and her two sisters, *Victorious* and *Vigilant*, have come into service since 1993. The fourth, HMS *Vengeance*, begins sea trials in 1999.

did not go quietly, and the US Navy owed him an immense debt, but he had become so autocratic in his final years that he was a serious enemy to any innovative thinking. With Congress willing to make the money available, a Secretary of the Navy who wanted the best, and no Rickover to intrigue against change, it was possible to make a fresh start. The new overall Maritime Strategy could be tested in war games, rather than by comparison of statistics, and new submarine designs would be evaluated in the light of their ability to execute the strategy.

New technology was also maturing. A new reactor was ready to go into production, the wide-aperture array (WAA) sonar and a new stand-off anti-submarine missile, the Sea Lance, were nearly ready. A new bi-static sonar (ie, with separate transmitting and receiving arrays) and new thin-line towed arrays (requiring smaller winches for a given length) were also in sight. The submarine community's

dissatisfaction with the 'Los Angeles' design was also a factor, expressed as a widespread conviction that Naval Sea Systems Command (NAVSEA) was hidebound in its thinking. Uncritical acceptance of assessments of Soviet submarines' performance was rife; everyone knew that the Soviet designers solved all problems with no penalties.

Demands for a much smaller SSN were soon dashed; the twin horrors of unreliability (anathema to submariners) and excessive cost (anathema to Congress) could not be negotiated away. Admiral Nils Thunman, Deputy Chief of Naval Operations (DCNO) for Undersea Warfare, set up Group Tango in May 1982 to discuss the characteristics of the new SSN. His main objective was increased firepower, nearly twice the weapon load of the 'Los Angeles' (up from 22 to 42). Thunman knew the new SSN would be more expensive, but he considered that acceptable if the new design had sufficient improvements in fighting power. Many discarded ideas were re-examined, notably the idea of improved steel. Previously, HY-80 steel had been used, but HY-100 offered 25 per cent more strength, and even tougher steel, HY-130, might be available.

SEAWOLF – CUTTING EDGE TECHNOLOGY

The design which emerged has eight launch tubes, positioned just ahead of the forward bulkhead of the pressure hull, and stowage for a total of 50 weapons. The machinery would be much quieter than earlier installations and more compact. The pumpjet propulsor would reduce cavitation, but even the slight reduction in speed would leave the new SSN capable of 35 knots underwater. The power output of the S6W reactor has never been confirmed, but it is believed to be not less than 45,000hp. The electronics suite would include the new BSY-2 command system, a spherical receiving sonar array, a linear transmitting array wrapped around the bow, the new TB-16E and TB-29 towed arrays and other sensors.

The new BSY-2 combat system was developed from BSY-1, but when the earlier system ran into severe problems in the mid-1980s it became a separate entity. It is the US Navy's first fully integrated submarine combat system, with all the sensors, data-processors, consoles and weapon controls riding the same high-capacity fibre-optic databus. The consoles can, therefore, be switched among every command or control tasks, and the bus can handle 1000 messages per second. The system software has over three million lines of code, so much

Above: HMS *Valiant* was the second British SSN, though unlike *Dreadnought* she had a reactor made by the Dounreay nuclear establishment. She was retired in 1992.

that in 1990 there was a risk that the program would slow down for lack of ADA programmers. The major system sensors are a low-frequency bow array, an active hemispherical array below it, a high-frequency array in the sail, the BQG-5 wide-aperture array, a long thin-line TB-29 towed array and a shorter, fatter TB-16D array. BSY-2 differs from its predecessors in the number of lines and frequency-ranges it can monitor simultaneously. All sonar output flows into array processors for signal-conditioning and beam-forming. The whole system is so complex that it requires 157 gallons per minute of chilled water to cool it.

The designation of the new submarine project was SSN-21, signifying 'SSN for the 21st Century', and if the US Navy's legally ordained hull-designator system had been followed, the first boat of the class should have been numbered SSN-774. However, when the name *Seawolf* was chosen, the hull-designator was SSN-21. To compound the error, subsequent names chosen commemorate states, previously reserved for the 'Ohio' class SSBNs.

Congress funded the *Seawolf* in Fiscal Year 1989, and authorised two more in the FY '91 budget. Almost immediately the Cold War ended with the collapse of the Soviet Union, and to many naval and civilian critics the Seawolf seemed an expensive, overspecialised design unsuited to the US Navy's future needs. The decision was made by the Secretary of Defense to cancel the FY '91 pair, and to run the

Seawolf as a technology demonstrator. Congress then had second thoughts, partly from real fears about the loss of the industrial base for nuclear submarine construction (as had happened when SSKs had been phased out), but equally from 'pork-barrel' considerations about unemployment in Virginia (Newport News) and Connecticut (Electric Boat). In May 1992 the second, to be named *Connecticut* (SSN-22), was reinstated, and later that year, during the presidential election Bill Clinton promised to support the case for the third. SSN-23 was ordered from Electric Boat in September 1993. The *Seawolf* was commissioned in

Left: The Royal Navy's 'Vanguard' class SSBNs have US-made D5 missiles and fire control systems, though the Chevaline warheads are designed and built in the UK.

defence budget under strain, and Congress demanding a 'peace dividend', such a total was unrealistic. The 'Ohio' SSBN programme was cut, and the treasured goal of a fleet of 100 SSNs was dropped. Critics argued that *Seawolf* was unaffordable, and demanded a cheaper design. The fallacy of these arguments lay in the fact that the dominant factor in cost would be overheads incurred in maintaining the specialised shipyards and sub-contractors. Previously, such costs had been spread over large numbers of submarines, but the reduced numbers would still be expensive, even if they are smaller, cheaper or noisier. There is also a baseline of capability; too 'cheap and nasty' would be a criminal waste of money.

THE NEW ATTACK SUBMARINE

In February 1991, design work was formally approved on a new 'affordable' project designated 'Centurion'. Its aim was to achieve a capable SSN at only half the cost of the *Seawolf*, close to the $600 million price-tag for a late 'Los Angeles' class boat (at late 1980s prices). Out of these studies has emerged the New Attack Submarine, originally shortened to NAS but now known as NSSN. Advanced funding was granted in FY '96, running through to FY '98, with building planned to start at Electric Boat at the end of 1999, and delivery in 2004. To compensate for the loss of SSBN work, Newport News Shipbuilding will share the work on the first four NSSNs. The submerged displacement is given as 7823.6 tonnes (7700 tons), while the S9G reactor and twin turbines will develop 24,000hp for a speed of 28 knots. The same level of quietness as the *Seawolf* is stipulated but weapon-load is reduced to 28, including anti-ship missiles, torpedoes and unmanned underwater vehicles (UUVs). A new combat system is already under development, a successor to BSY-2, with a single spherical bow sonar similar to the 'Los Angeles' class, and a similar conformal bow array. The core of the S9G reactor is planned to last the whole term of the submarine, a major reduction in through-life cost. As predicted, the cost of NSSN has not been contained; the last figure quoted was $2.6 billion for the first-of-class and $1.5 billion for follow-on units. We may yet see the *Seawolf* back in production when the implications of tampering with capabilities finally sink in.

May 1997, while the *Connecticut* will follow in August 1998 and SSN-23 in 2001.

The projected price was based on an assumed building rate of two or three a year, and one estimate was $2.8 billion per boat (including research and development), assuming 12 built. With the whole

CHAPTER SEVEN

Hunting the Submarine

Navies devote huge resources to defending against submarines, and the search for better means of detecting and sinking them continues. Since the end of the Cold War emphasis has shifted to the task of finding small conventional submarines in coastal waters, rather than hunting nuclear boats in mid-ocean.

From much of what has been written in earlier chapters it might seem that the submarine is invincible, and many submariners do indeed talk as if it is. But, during the last 80 years two out of the three major submarine campaigns have been defeated decisively. The two defeats were, of course, suffered by German U-boats in two world wars, while Japan was the loser in the battle against the American onslaught.

When war broke out in 1914 there were only two ways to attack submarines – by ramming them or by hitting them with gunfire. This did, of course, require the submarine to show itself, as there was no means of locating a fully submerged submarine.

The history of early anti-submarine warfare (ASW) is cluttered with a few hoary myths, but balanced by some bizarre ideas which were subsequently adopted. It has been said many times that the Royal Navy's solution was to send out steam picket boats with a

Left: The helicopter is vital in modern anti-submarine warfare, with its lightweight torpedoes, depth-charges, dipping sonar, magnetic anomaly detectors and sonobuoys.

brawny matelot armed with a canvas bag and a sledgehammer. The matelot would slip the bag over the U-boat's periscope, blinding it while he swung the sledgehammer and smashed the upper lens. Thereafter, so the story goes, the hapless U-boat would come to the surface and be captured, presumably by a cutlass-wielding boarding party. It is hardly necessary to add that no evidence has been found for this amusing countermeasure.

After the dramatic sinkings of warships in the early months of the war the Admiralty was pestered by a number of cranks peddling theories and inventions. We can dismiss the lady spiritualist who offered to indicate U-boats' positions with a needle and thread, but Admiralty records confirm that the use of seals was taken seriously. In the hope that these intelligent mammals could be trained to swim after U-boats, a number of seals were obtained from a circus, and trained to pursue a dummy periscope spewing out bits of fish. The scheme was abandoned because the seals became lazy and overfed, or exuberantly chased any noise-source in the hope of getting a free meal.

Above: For the past 100 years the torpedo has been a more potent ship-killer than the gun. Adapted to the needs of submarines its full potential can now be realised.

The depredations of the U-boats were too menacing for such diversions, and the Royal Navy was soon forced to define a tactical ASW doctrine, however crude it may seem today. The ram had the benefit of being just such a decisive instrument. When the light cruiser HMS *Birmingham* rammed *U.15* in August 1914 the U-boat was cut in two and sank with all hands. In October *U.19* had a lucky escape, when the destroyer HMS *Badger* ran her down at night, inflicting serious damage. A month later *U.18* was reconnoitring the approaches to Scapa Flow when she was rammed by the armed trawler *Dorothy Grey*. Seriously damaged, the U-boat plunged to the bottom and then shot to the surface, only to be rammed for a second time by the destroyer HMS *Garry*. This time there was no escape, and *U.18* sank after her crew had been rescued. The drawback to ramming was the risk of damage to the bows of the ramming ship, and all the wartime destroyers and sloops were fitted with a hardened steel spur at the forefoot to act as a 'tin-opener'.

THE FIRST ASW WEAPONS

Soon after the outbreak of war a number of destroyers were fitted with the 'modified sweep', a 60.96m (200ft) loop of wire fitted with explosive charges. The upper leg of the loop was kept buoyant by wooden floats, while a 'kite' depressed the lower leg of the loop. It was intended to be streamed when a submarine had submerged after being sighted, and could not be towed at more than 10 knots.

An electric indicator showed if any obstruction fouled the sweep, allowing the operator to detonate the charges. As it took some 20 minutes to deploy and because it restricted the ship's manoeuvrability, the sweep was heartily disliked by its operators, but it has now gone down in history as the first dedicated anti-submarine warfare weapon, and it is credited with sinking *U.8* in March 1915 and *UC.19* in December 1916.

Also issued early in the war was the lance bomb, a 9.07–13.6kg (20–30lb) charge on the end of an ash pole. They were intended to be used against submarines alongside, and in April 1916 the skipper of a drifter disabled *UB.13* by rushing aft and hurling a lance bomb down onto the submarine's casing.

The paravane was a torpedo-shaped device with lateral fins, and was towed from the bow of a ship to cut the mooring wires of mines. In that role it was very effective, but in 1915 it was adapted as the 'high speed submarine sweep', with two explosive paravanes towed from each quarter. In theory one of them would foul a submerged U-boat, which would detonate the charge, or, if the destroyer wished to get rid of them in a hurry, they could be detonated electrically. It was as cordially detested as the modified sweep, and also sank only two U-boats, *UB.18* in December 1916 and *UC.16* in October 1917.

Scientists were already at work trying to find precise ways of locating submerged submarines from the noise of their electric motors. The first non-directional passive hydrophones were issued to small craft in 1915, but they were inaccurate and required the vessel to be virtually motionless while the operator strained to distinguish any meaningful noise. Collaboration between French and British scientists promised much for the future, but the two unrestricted U-boat campaigns had to be fought without the benefit of their work.

By far the most effective ASW weapon yet developed was the depth charge, which appeared towards the end of 1916 in pitifully small numbers. In essence it was a massive charge of 300lb (136kg) of TNT or amatol, detonated by a hydrostatic device (ie, preset to explode at selected depths). From 1917, production was good enough to supply all destroyers and patrol craft with depth charges, rising from 140 per month in July 1917 to 500 a month in October and 800 in December. The *wasserbom* was disliked by the U-boat crews, who had to endure the concussion of near-misses during hunts which might last hours, during which light bulbs were shattered and blown rivets caused leaks in the pressure hull. In 1917 up to 300 depth charges were used each month, and in the last six months the monthly expenditure was 2000.

A variety of howitzers and bomb throwers was developed, ranging from 7.5in calibre up to 11in calibre, but these fired contact-fused charges, and were only effective against surfaced U-boats. By 1918, the famous destroyer-builder John I Thornycroft had produced the first depth-charge thrower, a stubby mortar capable of hurling the charge well clear of the ship. The first submarine to be sunk

Below: In response to the urgent need for ways to attack dived submarines, British shipbuilders John I Thornycroft designed the depth-charge thrower in 1917.

by a depth-charge attack was *UC.7*, attacked by the motor boat *Salmon* in July 1916.

Above: The death throes of a Vichy French submarine caught by a US carrier aircraft dropping a stick of depth charges off North Africa in November 1942.

DEDICATED ASW SHIPS

The most spectacular ASW measure was the Q-ship, a mercantile decoy commissioned under the White Ensign and armed with concealed guns. The aim was to lure U-boats within range by pretending to be a helpless victim. Elaborate measures were used to convince U-boat commanders, including a 'panic party' to simulate the 'Abandon Ship' routine. Although the Q-ships fought a number of heroic actions their successes were hardly decisive, and once the period of gun attacks came to an end they became even less effective. Several 'Flower' class sloops were altered during construction to 'Flower-Qs', along with a number of P-boats (PC-boats) but they remained regular warships, and their fine warship lines fooled very few U-boat commanders.

Soon after war broke out the Admiralty ordered a class of single-screw sloops for general-purpose tasks,

including fleet support as tenders, minesweeping and general escort. Named after types of flowers, they were followed by improved variants, and as ASW became more and more important their main task became the escort of shipping.

More specialised than the Q-ships were the patrol boats or P-boats, ordered in 1915 as the first dedicated ASW ships. They had an unusual low freeboard hull, destroyer-type machinery capable of 22 knots and a silhouette deliberately intended to look like a large submarine. Their light draught made them less vulnerable to torpedo attack from U-boats, and the large rudder and twin screws made them very manoeuvrable.

Mention has been made in an earlier chapter of the use of old 'C' class submarines and armed trawlers to

ambush U-boats. No fewer than 14 U-boats were sunk by submarines, mostly British, apart from the French *Circé*, which torpedoed *UC.24* off Cattaro in May 1917, and *U.7* and *U.96*, one torpedoed and the other rammed by another U-boat.

SCIENCE BEARS FRUIT

For many decades naval historians, particularly of World War I, tended to ignore the mine as an ASW weapon. The Royal Navy was handicapped by the lack of an efficient mine until 1916, when steps were taken to copy the German Herz horn firing device. By 1917 supplies of the new H2 mine were sufficient to start a major offensive against the U-boat bases in Germany and on the Belgian coast. The 20th Flotilla of converted destroyer-minelayers made frequent incursions into enemy waters, and in the final months of the war started to lay 'M-sinkers', the world's first magnetic mines.

A more enlightened attitude on the part of the Royal Navy towards science and scientists started to bear fruit in 1917, when the first directional hydrophones became available. By 1918, towed hydrophone arrays were in use, and two ASW trawlers were given pumpjets to reduce self-noise and improve hydrophone performance. By late 1918 the first ASDIC active acoustic sensor (the equivalent of today's sonar) was ready to start sea trials. Air power was also being used more effectively, and the large number of non-rigid airships ('blimps') operated by the Royal Naval Air Service. Although no sinking can be attributed to a blimp, it has been claimed that no convoy escorted by a blimp lost a ship. This is understandable, as the sight of an airship would make any U-boat commander dive immediately.

CODEBREAKERS

The role of convoy has already been described, and with its associated change of attitude on the conservation of shipping, it was undoubtedly the most encouraging outward sign of victory over the U-boats, but a much more insidious weapon had been at work since

Below: The same submarine, believed to be the *Amphritite* or the *Oreade*. Both were attacked on 8 November 1942 by aircraft of Task Force 34 during Operation 'Torch'.

early 1915. The cryptographers of Room 40 in the Admiralty Old Building penetrated U-boat ciphers to an extent which matched the achievements of Bletchley Park in the next war, and made the 1917–18 counter-offensive much more effective. Even Admiral Dönitz, writing about U-boat warfare in 1938, failed to appreciate the crucial difference made by cryptography. The commonly assumption that the U-boats 'nearly won' in 1918 could not be more wrong, and it seems more than probable that they would have suffered unbearable losses if the war had gone on into 1919.

Causes of U-boat Sinkings

Ramming	19
Gunfire	20
Sweeps	3
Depth charges	30
Submarine torpedoes	20
Mines (Allied and German)	58
Accidents	7
Other (including bombs	2
Unknown	19
Total	178

POST-WAR ASW

ASW is often assumed to have languished in the years after 1918, but even if budgets were cut much of the basic work had been done, and both the Royal Navy and the US Navy quietly set about equipping their destroyers with sonars. Other nations followed suit, but with varying emphasis, and as ASW was unglamorous it attracted very little attention.

The Royal Navy found that its Asdic-fitted destroyers were generally limited to 10 knots when sweeping an area, and then only in good weather. This meant that hostile submarines would be able to use their high-surface speed to alter the position relative to the convoy escorts. Although one or two submariners tried night attacks on the surface, where the escorts' asdics could not detect them, this innovation was not encouraged, largely because of the danger. The Royal Navy submariners thought principally in terms of attacking enemy warships, understandable because its likely enemies did not rely on seaborne trade to the same extent as the British Empire.

The Admiralty recognised the value of convoy, but was convinced that it would not by itself provide the answer to submarine attacks. A combination of convoy, Asdic and international agreements to limit the number of potentially hostile submarines was seen as the ideal solution. Unfortunately the financial stringency imposed in the late 1920s and early 1930s, coupled with a naive public conviction that another European war was 'unthinkable', made it impossible to create a strong ASW force. A modest programme of replacements for the 'Flower' class sloops was the best that could be done, but these designs were progressively improved until the basis for an efficient escort emerged in time for the naval expansion of the late 1930s. In the 1920s there was a large reserve force of destroyers, and it was presumably hoped that these could be hurriedly fitted with asdics and depth-charges in an emergency. However, by the mid-1930s many of these had deteriorated badly, and were unfit for the rigours of war service in any capacity.

Despite the proven record of convoy and Admiralty support for it, there remained a core of enthusiasts who promoted a return to the discredited 'offensive' use of patrols. This clique was only checked by the shortage of ASW ships, and it was recognised by the Admiralty that existing and projected force-levels were too low to provide full protection. While the public mood remained so unrealistic, and air power fanatics were intriguing for the abolition of the Navy, the Board of Admiralty was reluctant to make any case for increasing expenditure on ASW. The understandable fear was that the Treasury would insist on balancing cuts in other critical programmes. An unfortunate side-effect was wishful thinking about the value of Asdic as the complete answer to the U-boat.

The US Navy suffered from much the same problem. Isolationism was rampant, so any attempt to win funding for defending convoys between the United States and Europe would be denounced. The existence of a huge reserve of destroyers also bred complacency, the assumption that an ASW force could be improvised.

WWII ESCORT FORCES

In 1938 the Royal Navy was at last allowed to initiate plans to expand its escort forces. A cheap escort was designed, using a recent whalecatcher design from a commercial shipyard as the basis. In fact the vessel which emerged was a small sloop, but when it came into service the inappropriate name of 'corvette' was resurrected for it. So tight were Treasury constraints that the design was frozen, and could only be ordered after war had broken out. Plans were also made to arm fishing trawlers, and large orders were placed in Canada to mass-produce Asdic sets. To compensate for the shortage of destroyers a new type of small escort destroyer was ordered, and 20 old destroyers were modernised to a similar standard.

Above: The Lockheed P-3 Orion, the most successful maritime patrol aircraft of all time, and the backbone of US Navy, NATO and other anti-submarine forces for 30 years.

When war broke out a convoy system was instituted, and any doubts about Germany's willingness to undertake unrestricted warfare were dispelled when the liner *Athenia* was torpedoed on the first day of the war.

The fall of France complicated matters greatly, with U-boat bases much closer to the convoy routes in the Western Approaches. Between July and October 1940 the convoys' escort limit was moved to 19 degrees West, and the Royal Canadian Navy's Halifax Escort Force took responsibility on the other side of the Atlantic.

The loan of 50 old destroyers by the US Navy took some of the pressure off the Atlantic escorts, but they needed extensive overhauls. Although destroyers were popular for ASW they were designed for short high-speed dashes at an enemy battle line, and in the course of escorting a convoy, soon ran low on fuel. To remedy this defect many were converted to long-range escorts, sacrificing a set of torpedo tubes and a boiler to make room for more fuel and ASW weapons.

NEW WEAPONS AND TRAINING

New weapons were needed, particularly an air-dropped depth-charge, and a means of keeping a U-boat under attack without losing Asdic contact.

With existing Asdics the escort lost contact at the last minute as she ran over the target, and so the depth charges had to be dropped by guess-work. The Hedgehog was a multiple spigot mortar firing 14.5kg (32lb) contact-fused charges ahead of the attacking escort. Although the small bombs had no hydrostatic fuse, a hit from a single one would cripple a U-boat, and the explosion would indicate a success. Later in the war a triple mortar capable of firing depth-charges was developed called the Squid. An ultra-heavy 1-ton (1.02-tonne) depth charge was introduced to deal with deep-diving U-boats, and standard depth charges were redesigned to increase the sinking rate.

Training the large numbers of inexperienced conscripts was tackled vigorously, and in July 1940 a new sea training centre was opened to give intensive training to each newly commissioned convoy escort. Commanding officers resting between tours of duty were encouraged to pass on their experience, and to discuss with scientists their ideas for new counter-

measures. To counter the wolf-pack tactics two important devices were made standard, the 'Huff-Duff' high-frequency direction-finder and the centimetric waveband 271 radar. Both devices went to sea in the summer of 1941.

The entry of the United States into the war in December 1941 led to many more escorts being built, and American scientists produced a new range of weapons. The so-called Mk 24 mine ('Fido') was in fact an air-dropped acoustic homing torpedo, and its introduction in 1942 provided a deadly weapon against diving U-boats.

The increased efficiency of escorts was matched by improved techniques of airborne ASW. Better coordination between ships and aircraft increased the effectiveness of both, and the introduction of long-range converted Liberator bombers and small aircraft carriers finally bridged the mid-Atlantic gap. Offensive mining, particularly under convoy chokepoints to catch lurking U-boats, proved as deadly as it had 25 years earlier. But, once again, the most insidious weapon of all was cryptography. The massive effort of first British and then American cryptographers was concentrated on ASW, and without it the Battle of the Atlantic might not have been won.

ASW was equally important in the Pacific, but the relatively unsophisticated tactics of the Japanese submarine fleet made life easier for US escorts. The lessons of the Atlantic battle were applied with equal rigour, and Japanese losses reflected this.

POST-WAR PARANOIA

The situation after 1945 was totally different from that which prevailed in the early 1920s. The almost immediate disagreements between the Western Allies and the Soviet Union led to the formation of NATO for the defence of Western Europe and a series of regional alliances backed by the United States elsewhere. As Stalin immediately set about creating a large navy, with a potentially large submarine fleet, ASW continued to have a high priority for the US Navy and its principal Atlantic partner the Royal Navy.

Many of the weapon and sensor systems were late wartime projects, and there was no shortage of ideas. The driving force was the knowledge of the advanced projects found in Germany after the surrender, notably the Type XXI U-boat, the Walter propulsion system, and very advanced torpedoes. As the Russians had their share of the loot, it was certain that Stalin's new submarine fleet would before long reflect these advances. For both the Americans and the British, the unpalatable

news was that fast submarines would outrun the bulk of their wartime DEs and frigates. The answer was to convert a number of destroyers, whose traditional role in surface attack had virtually disappeared, but had the speed needed to pursue submarine contacts in bad weather. The US Navy began a long process of converting the wartime 'Fletcher', 'Gearing' and 'Allen M Sumner' classes, while the Royal Navy converted many of its destroyers to Type 15 and Type 16 frigates and designed a new generation of fast frigates. The wartime fleets of diesel-electric submarines were likewise given a new role as 'hunter-killers'.

NATO'S SOUND SURVEILLANCE SYSTEM

Until the mid-1950s sonar range averaged about 1371m (4498ft), and ASW weapons were effective within that distance. But new sonars like the US Navy's SQS-4 were effective out to 4572m (15,000ft) or even double that in good conditions, so a new series of standoff weapons had to be created. These included the US Navy's Rocket Assisted Torpedo (RAT), the Drone Anti-Submarine Helicopter (DASH), and the long-range Mk 37 torpedo. The Royal Navy produced an improved Squid, the longer-ranged Limbo Mk 10 mortar, and developed a manned equivalent of the DASH, flying light helicopters off frigates. The Canadians took this a step further, flying the much bigger *Sea King* off their frigates. But sonar performance continued to outstrip ship-mounted weapons, and by the early 1960s the SQS-26 sonar had a reliable direct-path range of up to 18,288m (60,000ft), and could in theory reach the first convergence zone at 640,08m (210,000ft).

The DASH system proved unreliable, and eventually the US Navy came to accept that the British and Canadian ideas on manned helicopters were more useful. The Light Airborne Multi Purpose (LAMPS) programme produced the Kaman SH-2 Seasprite (LAMPS I), whose modern equivalent is the Sikorsky SH-60 *Seahawk* (LAMPS III). The DASH and its British equivalent, the Westland Wasp, had been weapon-carriers, dropping lightweight ASW torpedoes on contacts detected by the parent ship's sonar. The advent of larger helicopters like the *Sea King* and the later *Seahawk* enabled them to operate as hunters and killers, using a dipping or 'dunking' sonar, winched down from the helicopter. This has made the helicopter virtually indispensable for modern ASW ships.

Until 1991, NATO conducted surveillance of the Soviet submarine fleet virtually on a daily basis. The linchpin of this was the Sound Surveillance System

(SOSUS), a series of passive receivers laid in secret on the seabed in the path of Soviet submarines' route to the Atlantic, which would have been their operating area if World War III had ever broken out. In a sense SOSUS functioned as Ultra had in World War II, enabling the ASW forces to localise contacts. The data picked up by the arrays was relayed to shore stations, processed and sent back to the 'pouncers' – the aircraft, ships and submarines. Over the years electronic data-libraries stored minute variations in the noise-signatures of Soviet SSNs and SSKs, and in its heyday the system could distinguish not only a 'Victor III' from a 'Victor II', but the fact that it was a 'Victor III' moving at 20 knots, and even, which 'Victor III'.

All submarines emit some noise, regularly from mechanical vibration, propeller-cavitation or external flow-noise, and occasional transient noise such as the opening of a vent or the bow cap of a torpedo tube. These noises are transmitted either as a spectrum, in which individual noise sources can be identified by lines at fundamental or harmonic frequencies, or as continual broad-band noise. Isolating, classifying and identifying these sources has been compared to breaking down the music played by a symphony orchestra to allow the listener to identify the individual instruments.

The improvements in 'array gain' (the minimum source levels which can be detected) made it possible to exploit the 'convergence zones' at which sound paths converge in the open ocean. This explains the massive increase in detection ranges in the last 40 years. Unlike the atmosphere, water is a hostile medium which distorts noise very easily, but it also allows sound to travel over very great distances. Unlike radar, which needs massive power output to increase range, sonar can achieve great range with low-frequency sound. The cleverness lies in the processing of the data.

The only drawback of SOSUS was that it committed ASW forces to a passive barrier strategy, waiting behind the barrier until a hostile submarine came through. The next logical step was to make SOSUS technology mobile, and this resulted in the passive

Below: The SH-60 Seahawk Light Airborne Multi Purpose System (LAMPS) Mk III is the US Navy's current shipboard helicopter. It can also launch anti-ship missiles.

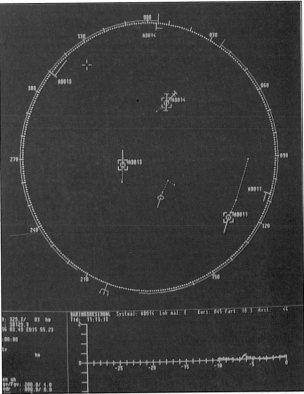

Above: Target Motion Analysis (TMA) allows a submarine to track targets using only passive sonar bearings. This is the TMA display in the CelsiusTech fire control system.

Left: The torpedo room of a British 'Trafalgar' class nuclear submarine. Data on each torpedo tube is displayed on the control panel (right) and relayed to the DCB combat system.

towed array. This was a joint Anglo-American development, in which British companies participated. Ironically, the use of the towed array in war was as a surveillance sensor, when HMS *Conqueror* stalked the Argentine cruiser *General Belgrano*.

At the beginning of the 1980s towed array technology was highly secret, but today these systems are primary detection sensors in a large number of submarines and surface warships.

LITTORAL WAR – A NEW SET OF PROBLEMS

In military technology no advantage can be guaranteed for very long, and as submarines become quieter, so the effectiveness of purely passive sensors diminishes. The hope expressed a few years ago that ASW forces had seen the last of active sonar has proved to be absurdly optimistic. Not only are submarines quieter, they have moved into shallow waters. As the SSK proliferates and the confrontation between the

Soviet Union and the United States recedes into history, so the new vogue for littoral warfare creates a fresh series of problems.

The SSN cannot shut down its reactor plant completely, so it will always emit some noise, whereas the SSK can shut down for a totally 'silent routine', and if the water is not too deep she can lie on the bottom. The SSK is also, as a rule, smaller than the SSN, so it can move in shallower waters, where noise-reverberation degrades the performance of all sonars. During the Falklands War the British ASW effort was directed to locating the solitary Argentine SSK known to be at sea. It was feared that she might be lurking among a number of old mercantile hulls scuttled off the islands over many years, so the area was 'carpet-bombed' with depth charges from helicopters and mortar bombs. In open waters whales provided a number of false sonar echoes, and more than 30 Mk 46 lightweight torpedoes were expended without result. However, claims that the ASW was unsuccessful cannot be taken seriously. Like anti-air warfare (AAW), the success of ASW

Above: The Augusta-Westland EH101 Merlin is the Royal Navy's new anti-submarine helicopter (due 1999). Its three gas turbines provide range and a large safety margin.

does not depend on submarines sunk, but on ships not hit. No British warship or merchant ship sustained any damage from submarine attack, so *ipso facto* the Royal Navy's ASW strategy worked. Lessons were learned, notably the value of the new generation of automated passive sonar systems (Type 2016), which reduced the workload on operators. The need for a 'weapon with a bang' was also demonstrated; a near-miss from a homing torpedo has nothing like the effect on morale of a continuous series of depth-charge explosions.

Although scientists have demonstrated a number of interesting non-acoustic methods of detecting submarines, including measurement of the 'thermal scar' left on the surface, and the minute differences in wave-height caused by the passage of a submerged submarine, these ideas do not perform well outside the laboratory. The ocean is very large, and subject to

constant variation through the effects of wind and tide, so minute observation of large areas is not practicable. Blue-green lasers offer some hope of penetrating the murky depths, but they are not yet good enough to replace acoustic sensors.

NEW SOLUTIONS

The maritime patrol aircraft (MPA) remains the strong right arm of ASW, armed with a variety of sonobuoys capable of providing directional information on submerged submarines, magnetic anomaly detection (MAD) gear and even 'sniffers' to detect the infrared signature of an SSK using its snorkel. The most successful MPA in service is the Lockheed P-3 Orion, which was built in large numbers and continues to be upgraded to keep pace with the threat. It has its counterparts in the French Atlantic and the British Nimrod, but nothing can equal the all-round excellence of the P-3. But MPAs are only as good as their weapons and sensors, and much remains to be done to adapt and develop the deep-ocean ASW techniques for the new type of warfare.

The mine still exerts its deadly influence over submarine warfare, and the new 'smart' mines are a very potent means of limiting the effectiveness of the most powerful submarines. The US Navy's Mk 60 CAPTOR (EnCAPsulated TORpedo) used a Mk 46 Mod 4 torpedo, which responded to the noise gener-

Below: Bofors Underwater Systems' new Tp 62 53cm (21in) wire-guided heavyweight torpedo (ex-Tp 2000) is fuelled by high-test peroxide for high speed and no tell-tale wake.

ated by a passing submarine. It is also possible to use traditional moored mines against submarines by laying them in deep water. Attempts to develop an Intermediate Water Depth Mine (IWDM) some years ago failed because of major technical problems, but the Russians, with a tradition of excellence in mine warfare going back 140 years, claim to have found a solution. The Gidropribor bureau in St Petersburg markets a Continental Shelf Mine, suitable for laying in depths from 60 to 300m (196.8 to 984.25ft). It is a development of the PMK-1 anti-submarine mine, which is in effect a launcher for a rocket-powered torpedo. On receiving a signal from the system's acoustic sensor the torpedo is released, reaching a speed of 60m per second (about 120 knots) over a relatively short range, measured in hundreds of metres. Its 300kg (661lb) high-explosive warhead can be detonated on contact, with a time-delay or by influence, and will sink the largest submarine.

A MODERN RETHINK

All the leading navies need to rethink their operational priorities and tactics. Although convoy has lost none of its validity, the worldwide trend towards smaller numbers of high-value merchant ships means that there cannot be vast collections of ships to be protected. Nor do navies have the large 'mobilisation assets' of large reserve fleets, and modern warships cannot be built rapidly. However, the underlying principle is still valid. The most likely place to find submarines is in the vicinity of their targets, and ASW forces are best employed in protecting small

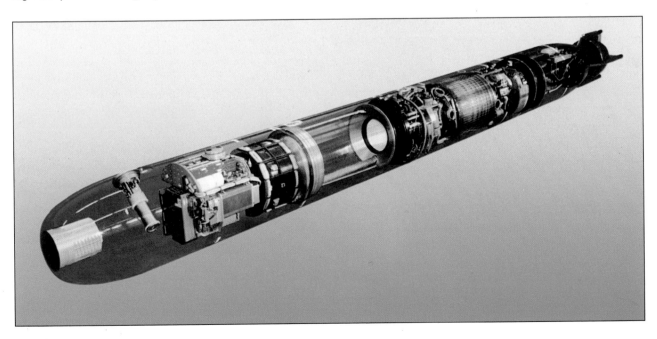

groups of high-value ships and task forces, not on 'offensive' patrols. Security and mobility are the principal aims of sea power, never more so than in peacekeeping operations. The old concept of 'Command of the Sea' may be dead, largely because of the SSN, but it can still be exercised over a small area for the achievement of specific limited objectives.

THE FUTURE OF THE SUBMARINE

As the end of the century approaches the submarine remains as threatening as ever. It is a deadly weapon of naval warfare, but it has never lost its sinister aspect, perhaps because successful submarine warfare puts seafarers deliberately at the mercy of the sea. Traditionally even mortal enemies knew that the sea was the enemy of all seafarers, but in some strange way, submariners ally themselves with that enemy. Certainly submarine warfare is not for the soft-hearted, as the crew of the *General Belgrano* found out.

Below: A South African Navy submarine scores a direct hit on a target, during trials of an upgraded heavyweight off the Cape of Good Hope. Even a single hit is very destructive.

The prestige of the submarine ensures that it will be owned by a growing number of minor navies, and its value as a deterrent will not diminish. Exaggerated claims have been made by submariners, who appear to believe that all problems of sea control will be solved if the budgets for surface warfare are reinvested in submarines. In 1981, a British Defence Secretary proposed to meet the Soviet threat by concentrating resources on a small force of SSNs and MPAs, and reducing the surface fleet to little more than a handful of small utility ships operating towed arrays.

It is a maxim of war that no 'dominant weapon' remains dominant forever. The worse the threat, the more urgent the search to find a counter to it, and a great deal of money continues to be invested in the search. If some of the non-acoustic sensors, terrestrial and space-based, fulfil their promise in the second quarter of the next century, the submarine could go the way of the battleship. This may be a bitter pill for submariners to swallow, but there is no scientific reason why it cannot happen. Until that comes about, however, the submarine and its hunters will continue to absorb huge resources, and it will continue to exert its influence over naval warfare.

Submarines at the Outbreak of World War I

By the outbreak of war the world's leading submarine-operators were already using a second generation, the bulk of the early pioneering craft having been discarded or relegated to training. Design and construction were monopolised by a relatively small number of firms. The rising tension in Europe resulted in a massive expansion of numbers, supplemented by wartime emergency programmes. The apparently large numbers of Russian submarines is deceptive; the diesels for a large number had been ordered from Germany pre-war and were never delivered. The list includes navies which did not become belligerents until later (the Italians in 1915 and the United States in 1917, for example).

AUSTRALIA

2 *AE.1-AE.2*	British 'E' class

AUSTRIA-HUNGARY

I-II	Lake type
III-IV	Germania type
V-VI, XII	Holland type
VII-XI	Under construction

11

BRAZIL

3 'F' class	FIAT-Laurenti type

CHILE

2 'Iquique' class	Electric Boat type. Became Canadian *CC.1* and *CC.2* in August 1914

DENMARK

1 *Dykkeren*	FIAT-San Giorgio type
6 'Havmanden' class	Holland type
6 'Aegir' class	Under construction

FRANCE

4 'Sirène' class	Laubeuf type
2 'Aigrette' class	Laubeuf type
18 'Pluviôse' class	Laubeuf type
16 'Brumaire' class	Laubeuf type
1 *Archimède*	Hutter type
1 *Mariotte*	Radiguer type
1 *Amiral Bourgois*	Bourdelle type
1 *Charles Brun*	Experimental
2 'Clorinde' class	Hutter type
2 'Gustave Zédé' class	Under construction
8 'Amphitrite' class	Under construction
3 'Bellone' class	Under construction
2 'Dupuy de Lôme' class	Under construction
2 'Diane' class	Under construction

63

GERMANY

1 *U.1*	Used for training
1 *U.2*	Used for training
2 'U.3' class	
4 'U.5' class	
4 'U.9' class	
3 'U.13' class	
1 *U.16*	
2 'U.17' class	
4 'U.19' class	
4 'U.23' class	
4 'U.27' class	
10 'U.31' class	Under construction
8 'U.43' class	Under construction

48

GREAT BRITAIN

10 'A' class	Used for training
10 'B' class	
35 'C' class	
8 'D' class	
6 'E' class	plus 7 under construction
3 'S' class	Under construction (Laurenti design)
4 'V' class	Under construction
4 'W' class	Under construction (Laubeuf design)
3 'F' class	Under construction (3 more cancelled)
1 *Nautilus*	Under construction (experimental)
1 *Swordfish*	Under construction (experimental)
7 'G' class	Under construction

92

GREECE

2 'Delfin' class	Laubeuf type

ITALY

1 *Delfino*	Pullino type
5 'Glauco' class	Laurenti type
1 *Foca*	FIAT-San Giorgio type
8 'Medusa' class	FIAT-Laurenti type
1 *Atropo*	Germania type
2 'Nautilus' class	Bernardis type
2 'Pullino' class	Cavallini type
1 *Argonauta*	Under construction
1 *Balilla*	Under construction
6 'Pietro Micca' class	Under construction
2 'Pacinotti' class	Under construction

30

JAPAN

5 *Nos.1-5*	Holland type
2 *Nos.6-7*	Kaigun-Holland type
2 *Nos.8-9*	Vickers type
3 *Nos.10-12*	Vickers type
1 *No.13*	Vickers-Kawasaki type
2 *Nos.14-15*	Schneider-Laubeuf type (under construction)

15

NETHERLANDS

1 *0.1*	Holland type
4 'O.2' class	Hay-Whitehead type
1 *K.I*	Hay-Whitehead type
1 *O.6*	Holland type
1 *O.7*	Under construction (Hay-Denny type)

8

NORWAY

1 *A.1*	Germania type, ex-Kobben
3 'A.2' class	Germania type
1 *A.5*	Under construction

5

PERU

2 'Ferre' class	Laubeuf type

PORTUGAL

1 *Espadarte*	Laurenti-FIAT type

RUSSIA

1 *Delfin*	
6 'Kasatka' class	
7 'Beluga' class	Holland type
1 *Kefal*	Lake type
2 'Karp' class	Germania type
4 'Kaiman' class	Lake type
1 *Minoga*	
1 *Akula*	
1 *Krab*	Under construction (minelayer)
3 midgets	Holland type
3 'Morzh' class	Under construction
1 *Sviatoi Georgi*	Under construction
3 'Narval' class	Under construction
24 'Bars' class	Under construction

58

SWEDEN

1 *Hajen*	
1 *Hvalen*	FIAT-San Giorgio type
3 'Ub.2' class	
2 'Svärdfisken' class	
1 *Delfinen*	
2 'Laxen' class	Under construction

10

TURKEY

2 'Abdul Hamid' class	Nordenfelt type (unserviceable)
2 'E' class	British design (under construction)

4

USA

6 'Adder' ('A') class	Used for training
3 'Viper' ('B') class	Used for training
3 'Octopus' ('C') class	
3 'Narwhal' ('D') class	
2 'Skipjack' ('E') class	
4 'Carp' ('F') class	
4 'Seal' ('G') class	
3 'Seawolf' ('H') class	
8 'Haddock' ('K') class	Under construction
8 'L' class	Under construction
1 *M.1*	Under construction

45

U-boats Sunk in World War I

This list, reflecting the modern research done by Robert Grant, shows the ineffective nature of the Allies' submarine countermeasures. From mid-1917, as the convoy system became more widespread, the losses begin to rise inexorably, but other measures, including a proper salvage and repair organisation, also played their part. In 1918 U-boat losses become unbearably high, and the belated mercantile ship-building programmes started to reverse the losses. The effectivess of mines should also be noted.

1914

9 August	U.15	Rammed by cruiser
12 August	U.13	Unknown (mine?)
23 November	U.18	Rammed by trawler
9 December	U.11	Mined
18 December	U.5	Mined

1915

January	U.31	Unknown (mine?)
21 January	U.7	Torpedoed by U.22
4 March	U.8	Sunk by explosive sweep
10 March	U.12	Rammed by trawler
18 March	U.29	Rammed by battleship
1 April	U.37	Mined
23 May	UB.3	Unknown (mine?)
5 June	U.14	Gunfire of decoy trawler
23 June	U.40	Torpedoed by C.24
2 July	UC.2	Own mine
20 July	U.23	Torpedoed by C.27
24 July	U.36	Gunfire of Q-ship Prince Charles
16 August	UB.4	Gunfire of trawler
19 August	U.27	Gunfire of Q-ship Baralong
30 August	U.26	Russian mine?
15 September	U.6	Torpedoed by E.16
24 September	U.41	Gunfire of Q-ship Baralong
20 October	UC.9	Own mine?
29 November	UC.13	Ran aground

1916

16 March	UC.12	Own mine
22 March	U.68	Gunfire of Q-ship Farnborough
5 April	UB.26	Caught in nets
25 April	UB.13	Mined
27 April	UC.5	Ran aground
27 May	U.74	Gunfire of trawlers
27 May	UC.3	Mined
27 May	U.10	Mine?
5 July	UC.7	Mined
7 July	U.77	Unknown (mine?)
14 July	U.51	Torpedoed by H.5
4 August	UB.44	Unknown (mine?)
21 August	UC.10	Torpedoed by E.54
27 September	UB.7	Unknown (mine?)
3 November	U.56	Gunfire of Russian trawlers?
4 November	U.20	Ran aground
6 November	UB.45	Mine laid by Krab
13 November	UC.15	Unknown (mine?)
30 November	UB.19	Gunfire of Q-ship Penshurst
6 December	UC.19	Depth-charged
7 December	UB.46	Mined
13 December	UB.29	Depth-charged

1917

14 January	UB.37	Gunfire of Q-ship Penshurst
22 January	U.76	Gunfire and ramming
8 February	UC.46	Rammed by destroyer
8 February	UC.39	Gunfire of destroyer
17 February	U.83	Gunfire of Q-ship Farnborough
19 February	UC.18	Gunfire of Q-ship Lady Olive
23 February	UC.32	Own mine
10 March	UC.43	Torpedoed by G.1
12 March	U.85	Gunfire of Q-ship Privet
13 March	UC.68	Own mine
21 April	UC.30	Mined
1 May	U.81	Torpedoed by E.54
8 May	UC.26	Rammed by destroyer

14 May	*U.59*	German mine
14-15 May	*UB.39*	Mined
17-18 May	*UC.36*	Unknown (mine?)
21 May	*UB.36*	Rammed by steamer
24 May	*UC.24*	Torpedoed by *Circé*
7 June	*UC.29*	Gunfire of Q-ship *Pargust*
12 June	*UC.66*	Depth-charged
7 July	*U.99*	Torpeded by *J.2*
12 July	*U.69*	Depth-charged
19 July	*UC.1*	Mine?
26 July	*UC.61*	Ran aground
28 July	*UB.20*	Mined
29 July	*UB.27*	Depth-charged
4 August	*UC.44*	Own (?) mine
12 August	*U.44*	Rammed
20 August	*UC.72*	Gunfire of Q-ship *Acton*
21 August	*UC.41*	Own mine
31 August	*U.50*	Mined
2 September	*U.28*	Explosion
3 September	*U.66*	Mined
5 September	*U.88*	Mined
10 September	*UC.42*	Mined
11 September	*U.49*	Rammed
12 September	*U.45*	Torpedoed by *D.7*
22 September	*UB.32*	Aircraft bomb
26 September	*UC.33*	Rammed
27 September	*UC.6*	Caught in mine-nets
29 September	*UC.55*	Lost by accident
Sept-October	*UC.21*	Mine?
3 October	*UC.14*	Mined
5 October	*UB.41*	Mine (German?)
7 October	*U.106*	Mined
14 October?	*UC.62*	Mine?
14 October?	*UC.16*	Mined
1 November	*UC.63*	Torpedoed by *E.52*
3 Novmeber	*UC.65*	Torpedoed by *C.15*
17 November	*UC.51*	Mined
17 November	*U.58*	Depth-charged
18 November	*UC.47*	Rammed
18 November	*UC.57*	Mined
24 November	*U.48*	Ran aground
29 November	*UB.61*	Mined
2 December	*UB.81*	Mined
6 December	*UC.69*	Lost by accident
9 December	*UB.18*	Rammed
10 December	*UB.75*	Mined
13 December	*U.75*	Mined
14 December	*UC.38*	Depth-charged by destroyer
19 December	*UB.56*	Mined
25 December	*U.87*	Rammed

1918

7 January	*U.95*	Rammed by steamer
8 January	*UC.50*	Mined
9 January	*UB.69*	Sunk by explosive sweep
19 January	*UB.22*	Mined
26 January	*U.109*	Mined
26 January	*U.84*	Rammed
26 January	*UB.35*	Depth-charged
January	*UB.66*	Unknown (mine?)
January	*U.93*	Unknown (mine?)
3 Jan-2 Feb	*UB.63*	Depth-charged
8 February	*UB.38*	Mined
12 February	*U.89*	Rammed
10 March	*UB.58*	Mined
11-15 March	*UB.17*	Unknown
15 March	*U.110*	Depth-charged
19 March	*UB.54*	Mined
26 March	*U.61*	Depth-charged
March-April	*UC.79*	Unknown
11 April	*UB.33*	Mined
17 April	*UB.82*	Depth-charged
21 April	*UB.71*	Depth-charged
22 April	*UB.55*	Mined
25 April	*U.104*	Depth-charged
30 April	*UB.85*	Gunfire
2 May	*UB.31*	Mined
5 May	*UB.70*	Unknown (mine?)
8 May	*U.32*	Depth-charged
8 May	*UC.78*	Mined
9 May	*UB.78*	Rammed
10 May	*UB.16*	Torpedoed by *E.34*
11 May	*U.154*	Torpedoed by *E.35*
12 May	*U.103*	Rammed
12 May	*UB.72*	Torpedoed by *D.2*
17 May	*UC.35*	Gunfire
19 May	*UB.119*	Depth-charged
23 May	*UB.52*	Torpedoed by *H.4*
26 May	*UB.74*	Depth-charged
31 May	*UC.75*	Rammed
17 June	*U.64*	Gunfire
20 June	*UC.64*	Mined
26 June	*UC.11*	German mine
4 July	*UB.108*	Mined
10 July	*UB.65*	Explosion
12 July	*UC.77*	Unknown (mine?)
19 July	*UB.110*	Depth-charged

20 July	*UB.124*	Depth-charged	16 September	*UB.103*	Depth-charged
27 July?	*UB.107*	Depth-charged?	25 September	*U.156*	Mined
3 August	*UB.53*	Mined	29 September	*UB.115*	Depth-charged
8 August	*UC.49*	Depth-charged	September	*U.102*	Mined
13 August	*UB.30*	Depth-charged	September	*UB.104*	Mined
14 August	*UB.57*	Mined	September	*UB.113*	Unkown (mine?)
19 August	*UB.12*	Unknown (mine?)	4 October	*UB.68*	Gunfire
28 August	*UC.70*	Depth-charged	16 October	*UB.90*	Torpedoed by *L.12*
29 August	*UB.109*	Mined	18 October	*UB.123*	Mined
8 September	*U.92*	Mined	21 October?	*U.34*	Depth-charged
9 September	*UB.127*	Mined	28 October	*U.78*	Torpedoed by *G.2*
10 September	*UB.83*	Depth-charged	28 October	*UB.116*	Mined

Austro-Hungarian Submarine Losses 1915-1918

Despite a largely obsolescent force and serious shortages the small number of KuK Navy submarines 'punched above their weight', inflicting heavy losses on the Allies, particularly the Italians.

1915

13 August	*U.3* (ex-*XXI*)	Gunfire

1916

13 May	*U.6* (ex-*VI*)	Trapped in nets

12 August	*U.12* (ex-*XII*)	Mined?
17 October	*U.16*	Rammed

1917

1-2 April	*U.30*	Unknown (mine?)

1918

21 February	*U.22*	Sunk by explosive paravane
6 July	*U.20*	Torpedoed by *F.12*

Allied Submarine Losses in World War I

The Royal Navy suffered the heaviest losses, largely because its submarines were offensively deployed in the dangerous North Sea and Heligoland Bight. Most French losses were incurred in the Adriatic, alongside the Italians.

FRANCE

Saphir	Mined 15 January 1915
Circé	Torpedoed by *U.47* 20 September 1918
Floréal	Sunk in collision 2 August 1918
Fresnel	Torpedoed by Austrian destroyers 5 December 1915
Monge	Sunk by gunfire 29 December 1915
Prairial	Sunk in collision 29 April 1918
Bernouilli	Mined 13 February 1918
Curie	Captured 20 December 1914, became *U.14*
Foucault	Bombed 15 September 1915
Joule	Mined 1 May 1915
Mariotte	Caught in nets 27 July 1918
Diane	Sunk by explosion 11 February 1918

GREAT BRITAIN

B.10	Bombed in dock 9 August 1916
C.3	Blown up at Zeebrugge 23 April 1918
C.26	Scuttled in Baltic 4 April 1918
C.27	Scuttled in Baltic 4 April 1918
C.29	Mined 29 August 1915
C.31	Lost by unknown cause 4 January 1915
C.32	Ran aground 24 October 1917
C.33	Lost by unknown cause 4 August 1915
C.35	Scuttled in Baltic 4 April 1918
D.1	Sunk as target 23 October 1918
D.2	Sunk by German gunfire 25 November 1914
D.3	Bombed in error by French airship 15 March 1918
D.5	Mined 3 November 1914
D.6	Torpedoed by *UB.73* 26 June 1918
E.1	Scuttled in Baltic 8 April 1918
E.3	Torpedoed by *U.27* 18 October 1914
E.5	Lost by unknown cause 7 March 1916
E.6	Mined 26 December 1915
E.7	Caught in mine nets 5 September 1915
E.8	Scuttled in Baltic 8 April 1918
AE.1 (RAN)	Lost by unknown cause 14 September 1914
AE.2 (RAN)	Sunk by gunfire 30 April 1915
E.9	Scuttled in Baltic 8 April 1918
E.10	Lost by unknown cause 18 January 1915
E.13	Ran aground and interned 18 August 1915
E.14	Mined 27 January 1918
E.15	Ran aground and destroyed 16 April 1915
E.16	Mined 22 August 1916
E.17	Ran aground 6 January 1916
E.18	Sunk by German gunfire 24 May 1916
E.19	Scuttled in Baltic 8 April 1918
E.20	Torpedoed by *UB.14* 5 November 1915
E.22	Torpedoed by *UB.16* 25 April 1916
E.24 (M/L)	Mined 24 March 1916
E.26	Lost by unknown cause 6 July 1916
E.30	Lost by unknown cause 22 November 1916
E.34 (M/L)	Mined 20 July 1918
E.36	Lost by unknown cause 17 January 1917
E.37	Lost by unknown cause 1 December 1916
E.47	Lost by unknown cause 20 August 1917
E.49	Mined 12 March 1917
E.50	Mined 1 February 1918
G.7	Lost by unknown cause 1 November 1918
G.8	Lost by unknown cause 14 January 1918
G.9	Sunk by accident by HMS *Petard* 16 September 1917
H.3	Mined 15 July 1916
H.5	Sunk in collision 6 March 1918
H.6	Ran aground in Holland 8 January 1916 and interned
H.10	Lost by unknown cause 19 January 1918
J.6	Sunk in error by Q-ship *Cymric*

	15 October 1918
K.1	Sunk by gunfire 17 November 1917
K.4	Sunk in collision with *K.6* 31 January 1918
K.17	Sunk in collision with HMS *Fearless* 31 January 1918
L.10	Sunk by German gunfire 30 October 1918

RAN: Royal Australian Navy; M/L: Minelayer

ITALY

Balilla	Sunk by gunfire 14 July 1916
Guglielmotti	Sunk by accident by HMS *Cyclamen* 10 March 1917
Jalea	Mined 17 August 1915
Medusa	Torpedoed by *UB.15* 10 June 1915
Nereide	Torpedoed by *U.5* 5 August 1915
Giacinto Pullino	Ran aground 30-31 July 1916
W.4	Sunk by mine(?) 4-6 August 1917

RUSSIA

Delfin	Sunk after being abandoned 5 September 1917
Beluga	Scuttled 25 February 1918
Peskar	Scuttled 25 February 1918
Shchuka	Scuttled 25 February 1918
Som	Scuttled 25 February 1918
Sterlyad	Scuttled 25 February 1918
Kaiman	Scuttled 25 February 1918
Alligator	Scuttled 25 February 1918
Drakon	Scuttled 25 February 1918
Krokodil	Scuttled 25 February 1918
Akula	Mined 28 November 1915
No.1 (midget)	Sunk in collision 26 April 1917
No.2 (midget)	Ran aground 15 October 1915
No.3 (midget)	Captured by Austrian forces 12 March 1918
Morzh	Lost by unknown cause May 1917
Bars	Lost by unknown cause 28 May 1917
Edinorog	Sank in tow 25 February 1918
Gepard	Mined (?) 28 October 1917
Lvitsa	Lost from unknown cause 11 June 1917
AG.11	Scuttled 3 April 1918
AG.12	Scuttled 3 April 1918
AG.13	Scuttled 3 April 1918
AG.14	Mined 6 July 1917
AG.15	Scuttled 3 April 1918

UNITED STATES

F.1	Sunk in collision 17 December 1917

U-boat Building Programmes in World War I

Despite the reputation of the Germans as the only fully committed submarine-operators, their High Command was irresolute, failing to standardise early and not putting enough resources into mass-production until the tide had turned against Germany. Thus their first unrestricted campaign failed to inflict crippling losses on the Allies because there were not enough U-boats, and the second precipitated America's entry into the war before the major programmes produced decisive results.

U.51-56	Improved *U.41* design
U.57-62, U.99-104	Improved *U.27* design (2nd group)
U.63-65	Improved *U.51* design-
U.66-70	ex-Austrian *VII-XI*
U.71-80	UE/UEI type minelayers
U.81-86	Improved *U.63* design
U.87-91	Improved *U.50* design
U.93-98, U.105-114	Improved *U.86* design (some cancelled)
U.160-172, U.201-212	Repeat *U.93* design (only 24 completed)
U.115-116, U.263-276	Project 43, none completed
U.117-126	Project 45/UEII minelayers
U.127-138	None completed
U.139-141	Project 46 'U-cruisers'
U.142-150, U.173-200	Project 46A (none completed)
U.151-157	Commercial design, but later armed
U.158-159	None completed
U.213-228	None completed
U.229-262	Very little work done by Armistice
UA	Ex-Norwegian
UB.1-17	Coastal type
UB.18-47	UB II design
UB.48-249	UB III (later units incomplete at Armistice)
UC.1-15	UC I type minelayers
UC.16-79	UC II type minelayers
UC.80-192	UC III type minelayers (only 25 completed)

Submarines in Service at the Outbreak of World War II

In the major navies very few submarines were left from World War II, and all existing designs were influenced by operational experience. The cruiser-submarines based on German ideas had largely proved unsuccessful, although a number of over-sized freaks were in service. Some navies, notably the French and Italian, had built very large numbers, to a variety of designs, but neither navy produced designs suitable for modern warfare until very late. The Japanese were convinced that the combination of scouting floatplanes and heavy gun armament would prove ideal for the Pacific, but the US Navy opted for a more cautious approach. Many more navies had acquired submarines after 1918, convinced of their value in coast defence.

ARGENTINA

3 'Santa Fé' class	Italian-built

BRAZIL

1 *Humaíta*	Italian-built
3 'Tupí' class	Italian-built

CHILE

6 'Fresia' class	ex-RN 'H' class
3 'Capitan O'Brien' class	British 'O' type

DENMARK

3 'Rota' class	
3 'Aegir' class	Obsolete
2 'Daphne' class	
3 'Havmanden' class	plus 3 under construction

ESTONIA

2 'Kalev' class	British-built minelayers

FINLAND

1 *Saukko*	Coastal design
3 'Vetehinen' class	German-designed Type VII protoypes
1 *Vesikko*	German-designed Type II prototype

FRANCE

9 'Requin' class	Oceangoing official design
4 'Sirène' class	Seagoing Loire-Somonot design
4 'Ariane' class	Seagoing Normand-Fenaux design
4 'Circé' class	Seagoing Schneider-Laubeuf design
31 'Redoutable' class	Oceangoing official design
6 'Saphir' class	Minelayers
1 *Surcouf*	Cruiser design
5 'Argonaute' class	Seagoing Schneider-Laubeuf design
9 'Diane' class	Seagoing Normand-Fenaux design
2 'Orion' class	Seagoing Loire-Dubigeon design
6 'Iris' class	Seagoing official design
15 'Aurore' class	Seagoing oficial design (under construction)
11 'Roland Morillot' class	Oceangoing type (under construction)
4 'Emeraude' class	Minelayers (under construction)
1 *Phénix*	Seagoing prototype (under construction)

GERMANY

2 'U.25' class	Type IA seagoing design
6 'U.1' class	Type IIA coastal design
20 'U.7' class	Type IIB
8 'U.56' class	Type IIC (some under construction)
16 'U.137' class	Type IID (under construction)
10 'U.27' class	Type VIIA seagoing design
24 'U.45' class	Type VIIB (under construction)
8 'U.37' class	Type IXA oceangoing design
14 'U.64' class	Type IXB (under construction)
03 'U.66' class	Type IXC (under construction)

GREAT BRITAIN

3 'L' class	Used for training
9 'H' class	Used for training
1 *Oberon*	prototype

2 'Oxley' class	ex-Royal Australian Navy
6 'Odin' class	Improved *Oberons*
6 'Parthian' class	
4 'Rainbow' class	
3 'Thames' class	Fleet design
4 'Swordfish' class	
1 *Porpoise*	Minelayer
5 'Grampus class'	Improved *Porpoises*
8 'Shark class'	Coastal type
15 'Triton class'	Patrol type
3 'Undine class'	Training type to replace 'H' class

GREECE

2 'Katsonis' class	Schneider-Laubeuf type
4 'Glavkos' class	Loire-Simonot type

ITALY

5 'H.1' class	
4 'Balilla' class	Odero-Terni-Orlando (OTO) cruiser design
1 *Ettore Fieramosca*	Bermardis cruiser design
2 'Archimede' class	Cavallini seagoing design
2 'Glauco' class	Ex-Portuguese
1 *Pietro Micca*	Cavallini cruiser-minelayer design
3 'Pietro Calvi' class	OTO improved Ballilla cruiser design
3 'Foca' class	Cavallini minelayer design
8 'Marcello' class	Bermardis seagoing design (plus 3 under construction)
5 'Brin' class	Tosi improved Archimede design
4 'Console Generale Liuzzi' class	
	Improved Brin design (under construction)
6 'Guglielmo Marconi' class	
	Bernardis design (under construction)
4 'Ammiraglio Cagni' class	
	Oceangoing design (under construction)
4 'Goffredo Mameli' class	
	Cavallini-Tosi seagoing design
4 'Vettor Pisani' class	Bernardis seagoing design
4 'Fratelli Bandiera' class	Bernardis seagoing design
4 'Squalo' class	Bernardis seagoing design
2 'Marcantonio Bragadin' class	Bernardis minelayer design

2 'Luigi Settembrini' class	Cavallini-Tosi seagoing design
2 'Argo' class	Ex-Portuguese
7 'Argonauta' class	Bernardis 600-ton type
12 'Sirena' class	Bernardis 600-ton type
10 'Perla' class	Bernardis 600-ton type
17 'Adua' class	Repeat *Perla* design

JAPAN

6 L3 type	
1 *I.51*	Used for training
1 *I.52*	
4 'I.53' class	
5 'I.56' class	
3 'I.61' class	
3 'I.65' class	
6 'I.68' class	
2 'I.74' class	
10 'I.76' class	Under construction
4 'I.1' class	
1 *I.5*	
1 *I.6*	
2 'I.7' class	
4 'I.21' class	
3 'I.9' class	Under construction
1 *No.71*	High-speed experimental design

LATVIA

2 'Ronin' class	French-built coastal design

NETHERLANDS

1 *O.8*	Ex-RN 'H' type, used for training
1 *K.VII*	
3 'K.VIII' class	
3 'K.XI' class	
3 'O.9' class	
4 'O.12' class	
5 'K.XIV' class	Enlarged O.12 design for East Indies
1 *O.16*	Seagoing type
2 'O.19' class	Joint home waters/ overseas minelaying type
7 'O.21' class	Seagoing type (under contruction)

NORWAY

3 'A' class	Obsolescent
6 'B' class	Electric Boat design

PERU

4 'R.1' class	USN 'R' design

POLAND

3 'Wilk' class	Normand-Fenaux minelayer design
2 'Orzel' class	Dutch-built oceangoing design

PORTUGAL

3 'Delfim' class	British-built Vickers design

ROMANIA

1 Delfinul	Italian-built
1 Marsuinul	Dutch-designed, built in Romania
1 Requinul	Dutch design (under construction)

SIAM

4 'Sinsamudar' class	Japanese-built coastal type

SOVIET UNION

6 'Dekabrist' class	Project 6 Series I
1 'Bezbozhnik' class	Ex-British L.55
6 'Leninets' class	Project 6 Series II (based on L.55)
6 'Voroshilovets' class	Project 6 Series XI
7 'L.13' class	Project 6 Series XIII
6 'L.20' class	Project 6Series XIIIbis
4 'Shchuka' class	Series III
19 'Losos' class	Series V, improved Shchuka
12 'Sterlad' class	Series Vbis
9 'Sayda' class	Series Vbis-2
33 'Shch.126' class	Series X
20 'Shch.135' class	Series Xbis (under construction)
3 'Pravda' class	Series IV fleet type
12 'K.1' class	Series XIV oceangoing type (most under construction)

SPAIN

3 'C' class	Holland type
3 'D' class	Under construction

SWEDEN

3 'Hajen' class	Obsolescent
3 'Bavern' class	Obsolescent
1 Valen	Normand-Fenaux type minelayer
3 'Draken' class	Seagoing type
3 'Delfinen' class	Minelayers
2 'Sjölejonet' class	Seagoing type (plus 7 under construction)

TURKEY

2 'Birinci Inönü' class	German design, Dutch-built
1 Dumlupinar	Bernardis design
1 Sakary	Bernardis design
1 Gur	German design, Spanish-built
4 'Atilay' class	German design (1 under construction)

UNITED STATES

1 'O' class	Obsolete
9 'R' class	
24 'S' class	
3 'Barracuda' class	Cruiser type
1 Argonaut	Cruiser type minelayer
2 'Narwhal' class	Cruiser type
1 Dolphin	
2 'Cachalot' class	Cruiser type
2 'Porpoise' class	Oceangoing type
2 'Shark' class	
6 'Perch' class	
6 'Salmon' class	
6 'Sargo' class	
4 'Seadragon' class	
12 'Tambor' class	
2 'Mackerel' class	

YUGOSLAVIA

2 'Osvetnik' class	Simonot design
2 'Hrabri' class	British-built 'L' class derivative

The U-boat 'Aces' of World War II

These figures include only those Commmanding Officers (COs) who sank 100,000 tons or more, and the tonnage totals are based on post-war research, not on the claims made by COs on their return to base. Note that many ships were sunk by gunfire.

NO.	NAME	SHIPS	TONNAGE	COMMANDS
1	K/kpt Kretschmer	44	266,629	*U.23, U.99*
2	K/kpt Luth	43	225,713	*U.13, U.9, U.138, U.43, U.181*
3	K/kpt Topp	34	193,684	*U.57, U.552*
4	K/kpt Merten	29	180,744	*U.68*
5	K/kpt Schütze	34	171,164	*U.25, U.103*
6	K/lt Schultze	26	171,122	*U.48*
7	K/lt Lassen	28	167,601	*U.160*
8	K/lt Lehmann-Willenbrock	22	166,596	*U.5, U.96, U.256*
9	K/kpt Prien	28	164,953	*U.47*
10	K/lt Liebe	30	162,333	*U.38*
11	K/lt Schepke	39	159,130	*U.3, U.19, U.100*
12	K/lt Henke	25	156,829	*U.515*
13	K/lt Emmermann	27	152,656	*U.172*
14	K/lt Bleichrodt	24	151,319	*U.48, U.109*
15	K/lt Gysae	25	144,901	*U.98, U.177*
16	K/kpt Kals	19	138,567	*U.130*
17	K/lt Mohr	27	132,731	*U.124*
18	K/kpt Scholtz	24	132,417	*U.108*
19	K/lt Endrass	22	128,879	*U.46, U.567*
20	K/lt Hardegen	23	128,472	*U.147, U.123*
21	K/lt Piening	25	127,649	*U.155, U.255*
22	K/lt Schnee	24	122,987	*U.6, U.60, U.201*
23	K/lt Bauer	24	115,983	*U.126*
24	K/zS Hartmann	24	115,616	*U.7, U.198*
25	K/lt Oesten	23	115,595	*U.61, U.106, U.861*
26	K/lt Hessler	20	115,040	*U.107*
27	K/lt Witte	22	114.378	*U.159*
28	K/lt Krech	20	107,450	*U.558*
29	K/lt Gelhaus	18	102,203	*U.143, U.107*
30	K/lt Rollmann	22	101,883	*U.34, U.848*
31	K/kpt Hartenstein	20	101,507	*U.156*
32	K/lt Jenisch	14	100,592	*U.32*

K/zS: Kapitän zur Zee; K/kpt: Korvettenkapitän; K/lt: Kapitänleutnant.

Nuclear Submarines Currently in Service

As the high cost of refuelling and decommissioning nuclear reactors became obvious in the late 1980s the numbers of nuclear-powered boats began to fall, particularly in the former Soviet Navy and the US Navy. The Russians have taken over 60 out of commission, and the US Navy's aim of a 100-strong SSN force has been abandoned. The two navies trying to design and build their own SSNs seem to prefer prestige to practicality, and both Brazil and India are making very slow progress. Russian warships are assigned Project numbers and in addition class-names, but during the Cold War NATO also assigned 'reporting' names, which are shown because they are better-known to non-specialists.

BRAZILIAN NAVY

1 prototype SSN planned

CHINESE PEOPLE'S LIBERATION NAVY

1 Project 092 'Xia' type SSBN
3 Project 091 'Han' type SSN
1 Project 094 SSBN under construction (plus 3 planned)
1 Project 093 SSN under construction

FRENCH NAVY

6 'Rubis' class SSNs
2 'Redoutable' class SSBNs
1 *Inflexible* SSBN
2 'Triomphant' class SSBNs (plus 2 under construction)
4 SSNs (projected)

INDIAN NAVY

1 prototype SSN planned

ROYAL NAVY

5 'Swiftsure' class SSNs
7 'Trafalgar' class SSNs
3 'Vanguard' class SSBNs (plus 1 under construction)
5 'Astute' class (projected)

RUSSIAN NAVY

1 Project 955 'Borey' class SSBN (under construction)
7 Project 667BDRM 'Del'fin' class SSBNs - 'Delta IV'
4 Project 941 'Akula'class SSBNs - 'Typhoon'
12 Project 667BDR 'Kal'mar' class SSBNs - Delta III'
10 Project 949A 'Antey II' class SSGNs - 'Oscar II'
2 Project 949 'Antey' class SSGNs - 'Oscar I'
1 Project 885 'Severodvinsk' class SSN (plus 6 projected)
13 Project 971/971U 'Shchuka-B' class SSNs (plus 4 under construction) - 'Akula I/II'
2 Project 945A 'Mars' class SSNs - 'Sierra II'
2 Project 945 'Karp' class SSNs - 'Sierra I'
18 Project 671RTM/RTMK class SSNs - 'Victor III'

US NAVY

18 'Ohio' class SSBNs
14 'Virginia' (SSN-774) class SSNs (projected)
2 'Seawolf' (SSN-21) class SSNs (plus 1 under construction)
54 'Los Angeles' (SSN-688) class SSNs
1 'Narwhal' (SSN-671) SSN
10 'Sturgeon' (SSN-637) class SSNs
2 'Benjamin Franklin' (SSN-642) class SSNs

SSN: attack submarine; SSBN: ballistic missile submarine; SSGN: cruise missile submarine

Diesel-electric Submarines Currently in Service

Despite the glamour of the SSN, large numbers of diesel-electric submarines (SSKs) exist. Although they lack the submerged endurance and sustained speed of the SSN, they can operate in confined waters and can be virtually silent. Boats marked * are equipped with air-independent propulsion (AIP) to extend the period between battery-chargings, a revival of German ideas. At least six AIP designs are currently on the market to meet the demand, but only the German PEM fuel cell and closed-cycle diesel systems and the Swedish Stirling engine have been tested at sea.

ALGERIA

2 Russian Project 877EM 'Kilo' class

ARGENTINA

2 'Santa Cruz' class (German TR1700 type)
1 *Salta* (German Type 209/1200)

AUSTRALIA

3 (plus 3) 'Collins' class (Swedish Type 471)
3 'Onslow' class (British 'Oberon' class)

BRAZIL

4 (plus 1) 'Tupí' class (German Type 209/1400)

BULGARIA

2 Russian Project 633 'Romeo' class

CANADA

(plus 4) 'Upholder' class
(ex-Royal Navy Type 2400 leased 1998)
3 'Ojibwa' class (British 'Oberon' class)

CHILE

(plus 2) 'Scorpène' class
(Franco-Spanish design, ordered 1998)
2 'Thomson' class (German Type 209/1300)
2 'O'Brien' class (British 'Oberon' class)

CHINA

1 (plus 3) Project 039 'Song' class
(plus 2) Project 636 (Russian Improved 'Kilo' class)
2 Project 877E (Russian 'Kilo' class)
13 Project 035 'Ming' class
64 Project 033 (Russian 'Romeo' class)

COLOMBIA

2 'Pijao' class (German Type 209/1200)

CROATIA

1 *Velebit* 88-ton midget

DENMARK

2 'Narhvalen' class (German Type 205)
3 'Tumleren' class (ex-Norwegian Type 207)

ECUADOR

2 'Shyri' class (Geman Type 209/1300)

EGYPT

4 Chinese 'Romeo' class

FRANCE

4 'Agosta' class
2 'Daphné' class

GERMANY

(plus 4) Type 212
8 Type 206A

GREECE

4 German Type 209/1100
4 German Type 209/1200
(plus 3/4) German Type 214

INDIA

(plus 2) Russian Project 636 Improved 'Kilo' class
9 Russian Project 877E 'Kilo' class
4 GermanType 1500
6 Russian Project 641E 'Foxtrot' class

INDONESIA

2 'Cakra' class (German Type 209/1300)

IRAN

3 Russian Project 877EKM 'Kilo' class

ISRAEL

3 'Gal' class (British-built German Type 500)
2 (plus 1) 'Leviathan' class (German 'Dolphin' class)

ITALY

(plus 2) German Type 212
2 'Primo Longobardo' class (Fincantieri design)
2 'Salvatore Pelosi' class (Fincantieri design)
4 'Nazario Sauro' class (Fincantieri design)

JAPAN

1 (plus 9) 'Oyashio' class
7 'Harushio' class
8 'Yuushio' class

NORTH KOREA

17 'Sang-o' class
22 Chinese Project 033 'Romeo' class
4 Russian Project 631 'Whiskey' class

SOUTH KOREA

9 'Changbo-go' class (German Type 209/1200 design)

NETHERLANDS

4 'Walrus' class

NORWAY

6 'Ula' class (German Type 210)
6 'Skolpen' class (German Type 207)

PAKISTAN

1 (plus 2) *French Agosta-90B** type
2 'Hashmat' class (French 'Agosta' class)
4 'Hangor' class (French 'Daphné' class)

PERU

6 'Casma' class (German Type 209/1200 design)
2 'Dos de Mayo' class (US 'Marlin' class)

POLAND

1 *Orzel* (Russian Project 877E 'Kilo' class)
1 *Dzik* (Russian Project 641K 'Foxtrot' class)

PORTUGAL

3 'Albacora' class (French 'Daphné' class)

ROMANIA

1 *Delfinul* (Russian Project 877E 'Kilo' class)

RUSSIA

(plus 1) Project 677 'Lada' class*
3 Project 636 Improved 'Kilo' class
21 Project 877 series 'Kilo' class
10 Project 641B 'Tango' class
3 Project 641K 'Foxtrot' class
2 Project 865 'Losos' class midgets

SINGAPORE

1 (plus 3) 'Challenger' class
(ex-Swedish 'Sjöormen' class)

SOUTH AFRICA

3 'Maria van Riebeeck' class (French 'Daphné' class

SPAIN

4 'Galerna' class (French 'Agosta' class)
4 'Delfin' class (French 'Daphné' class)

SWEDEN

3 'Gotland' class (A 19 design)*
4 'Västergötland' class (A 17 design)
1 *Näcken** (lengthened A 14 design)
2 'Näcken' class (unmodified A 14 design)
2 'Sjöormen' class (A 11B design)
1 *Spiggen* (midget)

TAIWAN

2 'Hai Lung' class (Dutch *Zwaardvis* derivative)

TURKEY

3 (plus 3) 'Preveze' class (German Type 209/1400)
6 'Atilay' class (German Type 209/1200)

UKRAINE

1 *Kherson* (Russian Project 641K 'Foxtrot' class)

VENEZUELA

2 'Sabalo'class (German Type 209/1300 design)

YUGOSLAVIA

2 'Sava' class (local design)
2 'Heroj' class (local design)
5 'Una' class (midgets)